TRUTH, TRUST,

AND THE

BOTTOM LINE

Also by the Authors

Diane Tracy

The 10 Steps to Empowerment: A Common Sense Guide to Managing People. (Harper-Collins/Quill).

The First Book of Common-Sense Management: How to Overcome Managerial Madness by Finding the Simple Key to Success. (Harper-Collins/Quill).

Take This Job and Love It: A Personal Guide to Career Empowerment. (Source-books, Inc.).

Bill Morin

Total Career Fitness: A Complete Checkup and Workout Guide. (Jossey Bass).

Parting Company: How to Survive the Loss of a Job and Find Another Successfully. (Harcourt Brace).

Silent Sabotage: Rescuing Our Careers, Our Companies, and Our Lives from the Creeping Paralysis of Anger and Bitterness. (AMACOM).

TRUTH, TRUST,
AND THE
BOTTOM LINE

7 Steps to Trust-Based Management

Diane Tracy | William J. Morin

DEARBORN™
TRADE
A **Kaplan Professional** Company

This publication is designed to provide accurate and authoritative information in regard to the subject matter covered. It is sold with the understanding that the publisher is not engaged in rendering legal, accounting, or other professional service. If legal advice or other expert assistance is required, the services of a competent professional should be sought.

Acquisitions Editor: Jean Iversen Cook
Managing Editor: Jack Kiburz
Project Editor: Trey Thoelcke
Interior Design: Lucy Jenkins
Cover Design: Scott Rattray Design
Typesetting: the dotted i

Published by Dearborn
A Kaplan Professional Company

Printed in the United States of America

00   01   02   10   9   8   7   6   5   4   3   2   1

Library of Congress Cataloging-in-Publication Data

Tracy, Diane.
   Truth, trust, and the bottom line : 7 steps to trust-based
management / Diane Tracy, William J. Morin.
      p.   cm.
   Includes bibliographical references and index.
   ISBN 0-7931-4163-X
   1. Industrial management.   2. Trust.   I. Morin, William J.   II. Title.
HD31 .T672 2001
658—dc21

                                                              00-011058

Dearborn books are available at special quantity discounts to use as premiums and sales promotions, or for use in corporate training programs. For more information, please call the Special Sales Manager at 800-621-9621, ext. 4514, or write to Dearborn Financial Publishing, Inc., 155 N. Wacker Drive, Chicago, IL 60606-1719.

Praise for *Truth, Trust, and the Bottom Line*

"*Truth, Trust, and the Bottom Line* provides practical guidelines that can help transform individual, team, and organizational relationships. This is a book that will not just be read. It will be used!"
—Marshall Goldsmith
Named "Top 10" executive educator by *The Wall Street Journal* and coeditor of *Coaching for Leadership: How the World's Greatest Coaches Help Leaders Learn*

"Management is about relationships. Amazingly, very few seem to know how to create and nourish them. The foundation is trust. The question is how to earn it. This book lays out the answer while providing pragmatic direction in a clear and understandable format. It is a career builder."
—Philip B. Crosby
Author of *Quality and Me: Lessons from an Evolving Life*

"Bill and Diane provide useful, meaningful advice from lessons learned. Refreshing and well worth the read!"
—Judith A. Norton
Senior Vice President–Human Resources, RH Donnelley

"How-to books these days rarely deliver on what they promise, leaving the reader with a vague sense of disappointment and annoyance. Although Tracy and Morin's book doesn't position itself to be of this genre, it clearly provides usable, credible guidance and insights for the manager-as-coach in helping people understand and achieve their potential. As the authors point out repeatedly, truth is at the heart of the matter, and this book, in an easily read way, takes you down the path of getting there."
—John P. Ryan
Senior Vice President, Human Resources,
Schering-Plough Corporation

"Many of today's managers see technology as the answer to everything. In this book the authors present an effective alternative by showing how to build the trust relationship between employee and manager. It is full of easy to use tools and tips to help managers improve their coaching and people management skills."

—Dr. John Sullivan
Head and Professor of HR, College of Business,
San Francisco State University

"Coaching is the leadership skill that results in highly productive people, teams, and relationships, and contributes to an environment that good people want to be a part of. Whether you are trying to attract, retain, improve performance, create a high performance team, or simply improve relationship skills, *Truth, Trust, and the Bottom Line* presents a comprehensive model for doing so. It combines a structured process for coaching with real examples and learning from two industry leaders in the field."

—Timothy T. Conlon
Corporate Director, Human Resources Strategy & Executive
Development, Xerox Corporation

Dedication

I dedicate this book to my husband, Peter Sage, the "coach behind the coach," whose integrity and compassion for people inspire me daily to walk the higher road.

Diane Tracy

I want to dedicate the book to the professionals of WJM Associates and to the 100+ coaches and counselors that work with WJM Associates.

I also want to dedicate this book to the people who are brave enough to offer advice and feedback to others, and to those who are smart enough to receive that feedback and advice and learn from it.

Finally, as always, I dedicate this book to my wonderful sons Mark, Timothy, and Jason.

Bill Morin

Contents

Acknowledgments

I thank my friend and mentor, Dr. David Bennett, who taught me to love the truth and how to speak the truth in ways that heal instead of hurt.

My thanks also go to Bill Morin who challenges me and helps me live the ideas we have written about in this book. Coauthoring a book can be a stressful, "messy" endeavor, but thanks to Bill's sensitivity and collaborative style, the process was always about the message and never about ego. His wealth of business experience and insights about people enriched the work immensely and taught me a lot in the process. It was a truly enjoyable experience!

Thanks to Maureen Klecha and Chrys Kasapis who served as resources.

Diane Tracy

My key appreciation is for Diane Tracy. She was and is an inspiration to work with and a great writer to observe. She is also fun, creative, brilliant, and lovely. How lucky can a coauthor get?

She is also the lead author of this book and toiled long hours in writing and rewriting the actual manuscript. I can't thank her enough for her dedication and hard work.

I also want to acknowledge the professionals I work with day-to-day at WJM Associates. They are Diane Amador, Jim Cornehlsen, John Finnerty, Judith Firth, Chrys Kasapis, Ray McKelvey, Jessie Peralta, Alidra Sims, Carrie Wilkens, Idris Braithwaite, and Jason Morin.

Bill Morin

Foreword

"Trust is the lubricant of society," wrote Kenneth Arrow, the 1972 Nobel laureate in economics. In my view, trust is not only the lubricant, it is also the glue that holds societies together.

When trust is present, when goals are relatively congruent, there is room for honest disagreement—an essential ingredient for innovation and growth. On the other hand, when trust is absent, innovation suffers and costs rise exponentially. Think of the games played with time sheets, time clocks, insurance claims, and expense accounts. No wonder economists are concerned about trust. It finds its way into all their calculations—whether the Gross National Product or the economics of the firm.

But trust does not spring out of a genie's bottle. It must be earned every day. Then it must be nurtured. So even though trust might be seen as a relatively soft concept, it must be grounded in hard facts and unvarnished truth. Lies, misdirection, omissions, exaggeration, even a string of white lies, destroy credibility. The words *trust* and *truth* are related to the same Anglo-Saxon root, *treowe*, so although one is seen as a soft concept, and the other hard or absolute, they are inextricably linked.

My own work has addressed both the conceptual and, to a lesser extent, the operational aspects of the links. But my work has stopped short of the contribution of Diane Tracy and Bill Morin in *Truth, Trust, and the Bottom Line*. Not only do they have a rich and comprehensive grasp of the conceptual issues, they have mastered the operational issues. With lively prose and case histories, they have demonstrated how, step by step, one can build, rebuild, or maintain trust within organizations. Not surprisingly, the primary tool they use is coaching. Both of them are executive coaches who have worked with CEOs, newly hired vice presidents, right down to first line supervisors. They have been tested in the marketplace. If their ideas and interventions had not worked, they would not have been hired and rehired by large, successful corporations, as well as midsize organizations, looking to energize their enterprises.

As I read their manuscript I found myself saying, "If I had read this book I would have been orders of magnitude more successful with employees, peers, and bosses." The authors provide self-assessment checklists and concise bullet points. Best of all, they recognize that, even though the seven steps they recommend are straightforward, the way to achieve them is sometimes a long and difficult path. This is a serious book—an important contribution. If you want to be a better leader, manager, or follower, *Truth, Trust, and the Bottom Line* will be a treasured resource.

John O. Whitney

Professor of Management at Columbia University Graduate School of Business

Author of *The Economics of Trust* (McGraw-Hill, 1994), and *Power Plays: Shakespeare's Lessons in Leadership and Management* (with Tina Packer) (Simon & Schuster, 2000).

Introduction

Why You Need This Book

Have you ever adjusted the truth, withheld the truth, or outright lied to one or more of the people you manage? Do you despise the job of giving your people bad news—particularly when it is about them? Is conducting performance reviews on your top ten list of things you most hate to do in life?

What about your personal relationships? Do you tell the truth to the people closest to you? Do you avoid conflict at all costs or do you let things build up and then nail them to the wall with your unbridled honesty?

And how about the reverse? Have you ever worked for a boss who rarely or never gave you feedback? Better yet, has a boss ever outright lied to you? Have you ever worked for a person who constantly spoke with a forked tongue?

Do you have people in your personal life whom you don't trust because you never quite know where you stand with them? Have you ever felt betrayed by a person because he withheld his true feelings until it was too late?

No doubt you know the price everyone pays when people can't talk straight and deliver feedback when it is needed. As a manager you also know that it is easier said than done—particularly in a time when top management keeps demanding greater and greater productivity, higher and higher levels of quality, all with ever shrinking resources.

Whom the Book Is Written For

This book is a practical guide for managers who want to learn how to tell the truth to their staffs and give feedback with positive results. If you think this is just another management book about the soft side of running a business, think again. As you will see in the pages that follow, the work doesn't get any tougher than this or any more important. Relationships are hard work; they are essential to just about anything we wish to accomplish in life that's of any significance.

This book is not just about coaching people with performance problems. We are so conditioned to think of coaching as remedial that we miss countless opportunities for helping people reach more of their potential. In the pages that follow, you will see how coaching can be used with your employees in a multitude of situations, including those in which:

- They don't understand their roles and/or the expectations—for whatever reason.
- They've just been promoted to their job and have a lot to learn before they will be able to master their jobs.
- They are new to the company and don't understand the culture of the organization.
- There is talk of a merger and they are fearful of what will happen to them.
- They are technically proficient and doing their jobs well but are lacking in interpersonal skills.
- They have negative attitudes.
- You have plans to promote them in the near future.
- You have given one of them a big project which is a big stretch for the person.

The list of opportunities for coaching is endless. In Chapter 1, we will talk more about when to coach employees. Hopefully, when you finish this book you will have a whole new view of when and how coaching can be used to further your goals as a manager and further the goals of the organization.

We wrote this book because virtually every day of our professional lives we coach executives who repeatedly tell us the same thing: No one in the company ever told them they had a problem. Or better yet, nobody gives them feedback about anything—good or bad. In the course of a year, we also conduct workshops and seminars for thousands of employees. The vast majority report that they receive little or no constructive feedback from their managers. Still others report that the old do-it-and-don't-ask-questions form of management is still alive and well in many organizations. The cost to business in lost talent, lost productivity, and lost innovation is staggering.

If it were possible to calculate in dollars and cents the cost of misinforming people and withholding feedback, we would all immediately elevate the task of coaching and counselling from the bottom of the to-do list to the top. Think of what it costs to lose one employee and what it costs to replace her. Think of all the unfocused, lost energy in the workplace because people don't know where they stand. Think of all the posturing and politics that occurs when people are on the defensive because of the withheld information and mixed messages they receive.

We wonder why 80 percent of all working Americans are unhappy about their careers (according to the *New York Times*), and why 46 percent of all workers worry frequently about their jobs *(Wall Street Journal)*. We wonder why we can't get people to *want* to come to work and give their best efforts. A study done recently by The Conference Board, a New York business research organization, found mistrust of management and low morale to be the most significant factors affecting employee-management relations today.

If you would like to build greater trust, develop and keep good people, improve performance, reduce errors, and cut costs, this book is for you. It is designed to cut through the mass of complicated management theories and buzzwords like a fine laser beam. It will give you a powerful management tool that will change your life as a manager and as a person. It will make you a leader in every aspect of your life—work, family, and community. It will help you understand the difference between managing and leading, between coaching and criticizing, and how to make the shift.

The tool is The 7 Steps to Trust-Based Management, which is simply a name for telling people the truth, talking straight to them, and developing them by giving them the information they need about themselves and their performance. It's a tool for coaching people toward greatness—theirs and yours.

The 7 Steps to Trust-Based Management are not complicated; they are practical and easy to apply once you know how. The benefits are immediate. They will save you an enormous amount of time and headaches in the long run. They are what the greatest leaders have been doing for years. We simply formalized them and put them into a format that you can learn, practice, and apply. They are tools which no manager who wishes to attract and keep good people can do without.

In addition to learning how to coach individuals, you'll also learn how to coach your team. Coaching is about connecting. You'll learn how to connect yourself to the team and your team members to one another so that a synergy is created—so that the team becomes more than the sum of individual contributions.

How to Use this Book

Throughout the book you will find sections entitled Our Experience, which provide accounts of some of our real-world coaching experiences—the experiences from which much of the content of the book was born. Many of the stories are about our work in coaching executives. Although you may not manage and coach executives, the coaching principles the stories are intended to underscore are basically the same for everyone, whether you are coaching an entry-level person, a professional person with no supervisory responsibility, a first-line supervisor, or an executive.

At the end of each chapter you will find a checklist which is designed to do two things:

1. Help you evaluate how well you are currently applying the coaching principles outlined in the chapter, and
2. Serve as a guide and reminder for the things you should be doing when you coach your people.

Hopefully, you won't read them just once, but will use them over and over on the job as you develop and refine your coaching skills.

The 7 Steps to Trust Based-Management can be applied to your personal life as well. Most of us have challenges in our relationships at work that are similar to those in our relationships at home and the stakes are high. With some minor modifications, this process can be used to dramatically improve the quality of your relationships with your spouse, significant other, children, parents, and friends. The results are greater peace of mind, more functional living, a reduction in stress, and more trust and respect from the people you care about most. At the end of each chapter you will find a section entitled Personal Application Corner which will show you how to apply these concepts to home and family. By the end of the book, you'll have a number of ideas for improving your personal relationships as well.

This book is based on the premise that people will not follow you unless they trust you and they cannot trust you if you don't talk straight to them. People can handle a lot of bad news but they cannot handle the painful ambiguity that comes from the lack of clarity about their performance and careers.

There are a lot of strategies you can use to scare people into submission without winning their minds and their hearts. But that's where the battle for talent must be fought today. The best people want and demand timely, effective feedback. High performance, quality, and customer service are direct products of honest communication and trust.

If feedback is so important, why are we so afraid to be direct and honest with the people we manage and in our personal relationships? How can we build relationships which lead to high performance? How can we dramatically improve our effectiveness as a leader, parent, spouse, and friend by dramatically improving our ability to bring out the best in other people? These are questions *Truth, Trust, and The Bottom Line* will answer. If you can discipline yourself to apply the concepts that follow on a consistent basis, we guarantee they will radically change your life as a manager for the better. Not only will your people be happier, less stressed, and more productive, so will you.

CHAPTER ONE

The "Coach Approach" to Management

Frequently in our work as professional coaches we are called in to help repair the damage done by an ineffective leader. In one particular instance we were asked to coach a new manager who was in crisis. In the six months since he had joined the company, he had lost eight of the ten people reporting to him which cost the company approximately $6.2 million in search fees, severance packages, etc.

When we conducted one-on-one interviews with the eight people who left, they each gave the same reason for leaving: They did not trust the manager. In story after story, they recited instances when he distorted the truth, betrayed their confidences, and treated them with disrespect. Through coaching, the manager eventually learned to change his behavior and develop more of a coaching style of management, but at a pretty high price to the company.

So what is a coaching style of management? What does it look like? We'll begin by defining the word *coaching*. Coaching is *the process of developing a relationship and environment through which people can discover their greatness, deal with their deficiencies and dark sides, reach more of their potential, and accomplish their work and career objectives.*

In any coaching situation, whether it is a boss-subordinate, parent-child, or mentor-mentee relationship, coaching is always an ongoing process. It is not event oriented—it is happening all the time. Coaching

1

is always about building a trusting relationship by giving honest, helpful feedback. It's about creating a psychological/emotional environment where positive things can happen. It's about setting goals and helping people achieve them.

Helping is the key word. In our coaching work we once saw a simple but powerful demonstration of what it means to be a good manager, a good coach. A boss and subordinate were having a conversation about the fact that the subordinate was not meeting the expectations for the job. Without consoling or criticizing, the boss simply looked the person in the eyes and sincerely asked, "What can I do to help you?"

Although the boss in no way relieved the person of his responsibility to improve his performance, we could see relief and gratitude on the person's face. In our own consulting business, we frequently remind each other of this story. By recounting it, we are reminded that far more is achieved by giving support and encouragement than by criticizing and condemning.

The relationship is the basis upon which significant change occurs. In order for people to engage in the tough work of honestly looking at themselves—looking at their good stuff and the stuff none of us want to look at—there has to be a vulnerability and there can be no vulnerability unless there is trust.

What we've actually just described is leadership. As one of our nation's finest leaders, General Colin Powell, said leadership is about mission and people. In a recent interview, he went on to say: "The only way to accomplish a mission is through those troops entrusted to your care. It's not you. It's not the organization. It's not any plan you have. At the end of the day, it's some soldier who will go up a hill and correct your mistakes and take the hill." He also posed the question of why you would follow someone around a corner, up a hill, into a dark room? "The answer," he said, "is trust."

Trust is an old-fashioned word that isn't used much in the workplace today. What is trust anyway? One way you know it exists is when a person asks you to do something without giving a complete explanation and you do it because you trust that person has your welfare at heart and wouldn't do anything to harm you. You believe in him or her. That kind of trust doesn't come easy and it doesn't happen overnight.

We once coached an individual responsible for $1 billion in sales whose people did not trust him. He constantly issued orders without any explanation or reasons behind them. Consequently, his people were always asking, "Why?" The executive expected blind trust from his people but had done nothing to earn it. He thought he was being expedient by operating in a military style but he was actually slowing down the organization by not answering people's questions and concerns.

Part of a manager's job is to work on people's competencies and skills so they can "take the hill," so they can accomplish the objectives of the job. That's the easy part. The hard part is getting people to *believe* in their own good stuff—getting them to realize more of their vast untapped potential. Most of us are much better human beings and far more capable than we realize ourselves to be. And most of us are clueless about our dark sides (and we each have one)—the destructive little things we think, say, and do in order to satisfy our ego's clever agenda. We unconsciously justify and rationalize away that part of ourselves which doesn't fit our carefully crafted persona—the image of the fine, upstanding, successful person who has it all together.

That's why we need a coach—someone who can lead us to our best selves. In the case of work, the person who is usually best equipped to do that is the manager we are reporting to. The built-in mechanisms designed to keep us from the truth about ourselves are just too strong. The manager's job is to help us look at it all, embrace the good and bad, and do something different so we can be a happier, more productive, self-fulfilled individuals.

Redefining Management

Although we have been using the word *management* rather freely, it's actually a word that needs to be deleted from business vocabulary. It is a stuffy, lifeless word; a concept that holds little relevance in the high-tech, fast-moving, dynamic world in which we are living. It's a paradigm that served us well when people were content to simply have a job and job security; when competition was based more on product and marketing than people and relationships; when change happened at human speed rather than the speed of light. Management as we have known it in the past is a paradigm begging for transformation.

Because the word *management* is such a part of our business lexicon, it's probably not going to go away any time soon so, the best we can do is to rethink it, redefine it. We'll be doing a lot of that in the pages that follow. We are going to undress it, take it apart, and challenge some of the fundamental beliefs that have driven the way managers manage for almost a century.

Interestingly, if we remove the letter *t* from the end of the word *management*, it becomes "manage men." (The word is so old that when it was first coined, women were obviously nowhere in the picture.) Think about it. The idea of one person managing another is a strange concept. The dictionary defines management as the act, manner, or practice of controlling. Perhaps that's why the word *boss* is a four-letter word to most people. No healthy, fully functioning adult wants to be controlled by another human being. If you don't believe it, ask your spouse or significant other.

When people are unhappy in their jobs, when relationships go sour, it almost always has to do with issues related to power, ego, and self-esteem. If managers in companies and organizations knew the true meaning of power and how to use it; if they understood the role of the ego and how much it seeks to be fed in most people; if they knew how to build the self-esteem of their people, productivity would soar, profits would skyrocket, and the competition would be left in the dust. In fact, anyone who understands these fundamental human needs and how to relate to them can just about own the world.

The Shift from Manager to Coach

Tasks, systems, resources, and initiatives must be managed and controlled. People must be encouraged, supported, and developed—in short, coached. When a manager develops a coaching style of management there is a shift in focus which enhances his or her ability to lead exponentially. Instead of focusing primarily on products and profits, tasks and activities, the manager focuses on people and relationships. It's a subtle but important shift. The manager never takes his or her eyes off the goal and understands the plays or activities that must be executed to get to the goal, but he or she knows that it's the people who are going to get you there; not technology, not systems, not marketing—the people. The relationship you have with them is the foundation. If they don't trust you, their energies will continuously be spent protecting themselves instead of continuously improving their performance. One eye will be on the goal and one eye on you—and not because you are particularly beautiful or handsome.

One fundamental difference between an old-style manager and an enlightened manager has to do with how he views and uses power. We once coached a young manager who believed that his job was to command and control. He soon found that he was surrounded by a number of people who did not respond well to this style of management and his career was coming to a screeching halt. His story is not unusual. For approximately 80 percent of all the executives we coach, this is a major issue. Our job is to teach them another way of getting the job done through a coaching style of management.

In the old, hierarchical form of management, managers had power over people. In today's world, the enlightened manager works from a different model. She works to nurture and develop the power within— the power within herself and the power and potential within the individuals and team she is assigned to lead.

One more difference: A good manager has his own ego in perspective. Instead of beating his chest and proving his own brilliance, he should be concerned with the business of helping other people shine—helping others develop a heightened sense of their own power and potential.

The most successful companies today are those which have made the philosophical shift from a command-and-control style of management to a coaching style of management. Not only have they made a philosophical shift, they are providing their managers with in-depth training on how to be an effective coach for the people they are leading. And they are holding their managers accountable for making the philosophical and behavioral shift.

Pizza Hut is an excellent example of a company which has achieved bottom line results by moving to a coaching culture. In the early to mid-'90s, Pizza Hut's share of the market had dropped substantially over previous years. In that period, a new management team took over and radically improved the company's financial results by developing a vision of a coaching culture and driving that vision deep into the organization.

They did more than send managers to a one-day class on coaching. They changed the manager and director titles to those of manager and area coach. Managers were taught a comprehensive process which, for one, dramatically changed the way the company identified, responded to, and solved problems. The process was designed to build and develop the people of the organization while building and improving the level of service provided to customers. Within 18 months, the company's market share and financial results improved significantly.

Management Paradoxes

Life is full of paradoxes and so is management. The better you understand them and live from them, the more effective you will be. Understanding these paradoxes is what changing the paradigm is about. Here's a list of just some of them. See if you can come up with some of your own.

- The more you focus on the needs of your people, the more the needs of the job will get met.
- The less you play policeman, the more control of the work you will have.
- The less you remind people of your power, the more power you will have to get the job done.
- The more you help people feel good about themselves, the better they will feel about you.
- The less you command and demand, the more willing they will be to do the job.

Many of us have worked under a very different paradigm. And for most of us, unless we have had some type of intervention or are particularly enlightened, we just simply pass on what has been done to us—what we have seen modelled. Working under the coaching paradigm is so much easier, so much more enjoyable. Work is transformed into play; energy that was spent posturing, politicking, and manipulating is now put toward the work. Everyone gets liberated—especially you, the manager.

Coaching Conditions

Our definition of coaching can apply to almost any situation but when we apply it to work, the process takes place for the purpose of helping the individual fulfill the responsibilities, meet the standards and expectations, and accomplish the goals and objectives of the job.

In order for this to happen, certain things must be in place if the coaching is to be effective.

- The job must be clearly defined.

- The person must be suited for the job in terms of competencies, experience, education, etc.
- The standards and expectations must be set and communicated to the person.
- The person should have clearly defined goals and objectives against which she will be evaluated.

This book is about the feedback process which should take place between a manager and the individuals reporting to him. In order to be effective, this process should be supported by the company's formal feedback policy and procedure which is beyond the scope of this book. Managers must be held accountable for giving feedback to their people in a timely, constructive manner.

There are other things that must be in place in order for a person to grow and develop on the job but if these are not present, any type of coaching effort will fail.

Common Misconceptions about Coaching

Coaching is one of those words that's been around for a while and consequently has some baggage. For many of us, coaching conjures up images of sports. There's a lot we can learn from famous sports coaches but to make direct translations to business can be dangerous because the playing field is so different.

To have a coach today has become somewhat trendy. People have fitness coaches, career coaches, communication coaches, image coaches—you name it and there's a coach for it. Whenever something becomes a trend or a fad, there are usually a fair amount of misconceptions about what it really means. When everyone is trying to make a buck off the new trend, the true meaning of the word or concept often gets lost in the hulabaloo.

When we refer to coaching in this book we are referring to good sound leadership and management. The 7 Steps to Trust-Based Management process which we will introduce shortly can be applied to managers, supervisors, team leaders, internal consultants, and professional coaches as well. Most of the principles, with minor modifications, can also be applied to other situations, such as parenting, mentoring, etc.

So what are some of the common misconceptions about coaching in the workplace? Here's a list of some of them.

- *Coaching is primarily for correcting behavior.* If we only coach people when they do something wrong, we have missed the point. The focus should be on what people are capable of doing and being, and then working toward that end. It's about *building* not *fixing*.
- *Coaching requires giving up power and control.* When a manager adopts a coaching style of management the manager doesn't give up her formal authority but uses it sparingly—the manager relies more on influence. The person is still accountable but the manager gets more control of the work product by being less controlling of the people.
- *Coaching takes too much time.* Coaching takes too much time if you don't do enough of it and you don't do it correctly. In either case, you won't get the benefits that come from effective coaching and it will feel like a waste of time.
- *Coaching is soft stuff.* The manager who avoids the soft stuff usually does so because it is so hard—the work is easy, people are difficult. Because the people stuff is so hard, the ill-equipped manager minimizes its importance and labels it soft. That's probably why a lot of workaholics put so many hours in at the office. Work is easier to deal with than home and family.
- *Coaching is laissez-faire management.* When we talk about focusing on people and relationships we are not talking about being easy on people or indulging them. Nor are we talking about letting them run the show. Coaching is about empowering people and helping them more fully utilize their talent and abilities. Here's another management paradox for you: Freedom in the workplace, actually just about anywhere, is rooted in strict discipline. The disciplines—telling people their jobs, laying out the expectations, giving them feedback, holding them accountable—are the things that enable people to reach more of their potential in the context of the job. In fact, it's only through effective coaching and discipline that a manager earns the right to expect excellence from people.
- *Coaching is simply being a good cheerleader.* A good manager is a cheerleader but it doesn't stop there. A good manager has the courage and inner strength when needed to tell people the truth—to deliver bad news. Coaching is not just patting people on the back.

Sometimes it is kicking them in the butt. It is always done with the express purpose of helping the person.

- *Coaching is like therapy.* Coaching is about understanding people without getting into their deep dark secrets, personal problems, or childhood. To be a good manager and coach one does need a basic understanding of human behavior and motivation, but therapy has no place in your relationship with the people you are leading. First of all, most people are not trained to play that role, and even if you were, it's not appropriate for the workplace. You want to encourage people to be self-reflective, but diving too deep into their psyche can be dangerous. Don't go there!

- *Coaching is telling people what to do.* You are the manager so you must know more, right? Not necessarily so. And even if you do, people don't usually learn from being told something. They learn best through self-discovery. When you tell somebody something, regardless of how brilliant it is, it is like a flicker of light passing through his gray matter. When people discover something for themselves it is like a brilliant lightbulb that goes off in their heads. Your job is to get them connected to the circuit. Yes, there will be times when you must tell a person to do something, but those times should be restricted to the times when you are delegating work or in an emergency.

▼OUR EXPERIENCE

What You Don't Tell Them Can Hurt You . . . and Them

It's amazing how many successful, high-level executives just don't get it. They may be brilliant business people but when it comes to understanding and managing people, one wonders how they ever got to where they are.

Once when I was coaching an upper-middle manager in a well-known Fortune 500 company, I met with the person's boss as I do periodically when I am serving as an external coach. Upon meeting with me, the boss proceeded to tell me all the things about the person that he didn't like. His dislike for my coachee was so intense that almost everything about him was bothersome—right down to the way he parted his hair.

Interestingly, my coachee was extremely bright, talented, experienced, and capable—someone the company did not want to lose, which incidentally, is why they spent the resources to hire an outside coach for him. But, like all of us he had some quirks—quirks which evidently pushed the boss's buttons big time. When I asked the boss if he had ever shared his concerns with the coachee, if he had ever given him feedback, his reply was: "No. If I criticized him I wouldn't be acting as a positive leader, would I?" This high-level executive did not understand one of the most basic management principles: If you don't give people feedback, they will keep doing the same irritating things. We think people know what they are doing. People can't change unless you tell them. Withholding information from a person is a disservice to everyone.

Because the boss had what we call feedback back-up—stuff he had not gotten off his chest or out of his system—it was poisoning the relationship. His unexpressed dissatisfaction with the person kept him from seeing his positive qualities. In fact, his negative impressions of the person were so strong, I asked him if he thought he would be able to even recognize the positive changes if and when they occurred.

The story has a happy ending. The coachee worked very hard on his issues, the boss stayed open and looked for the positive change, and eight months later he was promoted. Needless to say, the boss is no longer bothered by how he parts his hair. It's safe to say that without coaching, the company would have lost a very valuable person.

—Diane

Truth or Consequences

Remember the old game show *Truth or Consequences* (post–baby boomers probably won't) where people either told the truth or lied and paid a consequence? That's how it is with coaching. You either pay now or pay later.

Honesty is at the heart of the coaching process. It's the manager's stock and trade. Without it, coaching becomes at best a game, a waste of time. Your skills in coaching will depend heavily on your ability to get to the truth about a lot of things—the person, her strengths and weaknesses, problems and challenges, etc. The truth is what you are after. Once you are confident that you see the picture clearly, you have to be able to deliver the truth in such a way that the person is able to hear it and embrace it—sometimes a difficult task.

Many people in the workplace are afraid to tell the truth—to anyone. They do everything possible to avoid confrontation. Most of us who have worked for any length of time know of someone who was punished for speaking the truth. And it's not just managers who do the punishing. Employees can be quite skillful in how they punish managers for telling the truth: shutting down, talking behind the manager's back, sabotaging the work; the list goes on. And if the new 360-degree feedback process is not handled properly, it becomes one more way employees can punish managers. (In case you are unfamiliar with the 360-degree feedback process, it is a process whereby a person gets feedback from superiors, peers, and subordinates [if the person is a manager]. The idea is to get a better, more accurate picture of the person's strengths and weaknesses by getting the perspectives of a number of different people who work with the person.)

Some people are so fearful of rejection that they tell others what they want to hear rather than what they think and feel. Managers who suffer from low self-esteem and a weak ego are often the last to tell employees the truth because they are afraid of what they might get back—some information about themselves as a manager which they cannot bear to hear.

Still others were taught somewhere that they are responsible for other people's feelings so they go through life protecting others at the expense of their own truth and integrity. Whatever the reason for withholding the truth, and there are many, the consequences are always high. Here's one more paradox: We have this idea that if we tell the truth we will break the relationship, which is exactly what happens when we don't tell the truth. The relationship breaks because it is based on lies; lies which sooner or later must face the light of day.

Telling the truth, of course, must always involve discretion, timeliness, and good intentions. Otherwise, telling the truth becomes a weapon for hurting others and achieving self-serving goals—all in the name of honesty. Honesty is like fire. It can either warm and inspire people or it can burn and destroy them.

When we speak of telling the truth as a manager we are referring to those things that matter to the person, to the relationship, to the job, to the customer, and to the company. When we withhold the truth about important things, the important things become a barrier to the relationship and the work. If you've ever withheld the truth from an employee whom you liked and didn't want to hurt, only to explode one day because you just couldn't stand some aspect of his behavior or performance one more second, then you know the price you pay in terms of the relationship and the employee's morale when you don't tell the truth in a timely manner.

This is why coaching is the hard stuff because it involves telling the truth. It takes courage to tell the truth. Most of us have been so programmed to withhold the truth, water it down, or outright lie that we don't know how to do it—and we are afraid to try because the few times we have tried it backfired.

In the pages that follow we are going to replace your fear of telling the truth with insight and skill. Remember in the Jim Carrey movie *Liar, Liar* when he is forced to tell the truth as a result of a wish his young son made? He proceeds to tell everybody the whole truth and nothing but the truth. He goes from editing everything that goes through his mind to editing nothing and it is met with disastrous results. That's not what we are after.

The Question of Time

If coaching is an ongoing process, how does a manager find the time to do anything else? There are still meetings to attend, projects to lead, reports to complete—you know the list. The problem of time is multiplied by the number of people and/or teams a manager is assigned to lead.

Well, it's similar to parenting. The parenting never stops but it takes a number of different forms. Just like parenting is more than periodic heart-to-hearts, coaching is more than periodic coaching sessions. Your one-on-one coaching sessions or meetings are certainly one of the fundamental elements of the coaching process. Through these sessions the manager comes to metabolize his or her work experiences and learn from them. The coaching sessions, however, are only one part of the process.

One of your primary jobs as a manager is to teach people how to be their own coach when you are not there. One of your first challenges is to get people excited about their own growth and development—to give them a curiosity about themselves. Once you get them past the fear of looking at their imperfections, which we will talk more about later, the process can be quite satisfying and rewarding.

When people feel the sense of empowerment that comes from understanding one's self, taking full ownership of one's gifts and gaffes, and then changing themselves for the better, the process takes on a whole new meaning and spirit—for you and the people you are leading.

The idea is to help people develop skills for self-reflection and self-understanding. The same or similar thought process you go through during your one-on-one meetings will, hopefully, be used by the person when you are not around.

Part of your job is to orchestrate opportunities for learning and growth. These opportunities could take any number of forms. In fact, the more varied the better. Sometimes they may not be directly connected to work. You may, for example, suggest to the person that she see a certain movie—a movie that communicates a powerful message—that relates to something the coachee is struggling with in her interpersonal relationships at work.

Those learning opportunities may consist of some of the more traditional ones, such as taking a course or meeting with a particular person. Again, the more creative you can be, the better. You need a big bag of tricks and techniques because what works with one person may not work for another.

And, of course, it goes without saying, no matter who you are, the example you set is a constant form of coaching. When you model the very things you suggest to the person, he gets to see the concepts in action and the results. And remember, your relationship is the basis upon which the change will occur.

When Coaching Is Called for

As we mentioned in the Introduction, we are so conditioned to think of coaching as remedial that we miss countless opportunities for helping people reach more of their potential. The adage "if it ain't broke, don't fix it" does not apply to people. Not that you are going to fix people, but it's not enough to simply leave them alone as long as they aren't screwing up. There are a multitude of situations where coaching is not only appropriate but very much needed.

Here is a partial list that includes the situations listed in the Introduction (we know some people skip the introduction of a book which is why we are repeating ourselves).

- They don't understand their roles and/or the expectations—for whatever reason.

- They've just been promoted to their jobs and have a lot to learn before they will be able to master their jobs.
- They are new to the company and don't understand the culture of the organization.
- There is talk of a merger and they are fearful of what will happen to them.
- They are technically proficient but are lacking in interpersonal skills.
- They have negative attitudes.
- You sense they have some issues with you and/or upper management and you aren't sure what the issues are.
- They have a lot of talent and are meeting the job standards but performing much below their capacity.
- You have plans to promote them in the near future.
- You observe a change in attitude and/or demeanor.
- You fear they may be looking for other jobs and you don't want to lose them.
- They've worked especially hard on a recent project and they need some extra attention and recognition.
- Some new systems are being implemented and there is no formal training program to bring them up to speed.
- You've given them a large project which is a big stretch for them.
- You sense they are getting burned out.
- Resources have been taken away so they have to invent new ways to get the job done.
- They are upset by recent organizational changes.

The opportunities for coaching are limitless, as you can see. No, it isn't your job to play mind reader, nor is it your job to be their parent, but it *is* your job to constantly sniff out potential problems and be alert to opportunities. Unfortunately, many people won't come and tell you directly that they are unhappy or they have a problem. You have to almost develop a sixth sense for knowing when a person needs some attention.

▼OUR EXPERIENCE
Coaching Is not Always the Solution

Once I was asked by a company to coach an executive who was notorious for making sexist comments. He had a long history of such behavior.

It had been brought to his attention on many occasions and it was even noted in his human resource file.

In this situation, termination is the solution, not coaching. Coaching would have been appropriate when the executive first began making such comments but when he was advised time and again to change his behavior and he did not, he should have been terminated. When management lets such behavior go unaddressed without consequence it sends a loud message to the rest of the organization. It says management condones the behavior and doesn't care how it affects others.
—Bill

How to Know if Coaching Is the Solution

Let's say you do have a performance problem with a person. She is not meeting the quality standards you have set. Here are some of the questions you are going to ask before you even schedule a coaching session.

- What is the performance problem? Can you tell the subordinate exactly what you want her to change?
- Is it worth your time? All employees have faults and they will never be perfect. Coaching takes time. Is this behavior lapse worth the effort?
- Does the person know her behavior is not what it should be? Sometimes people just need to be made aware of the situation.
- Is this behavior change something the person is capable of? Is the person suited for the job? If it's a capacity problem, coaching won't help.
- Are there obstacles to performance that are beyond the person's control? It may be necessary to change the system instead of the employee.
- Are the rewards shaping the behavior? Do positive rewards follow good performance? Is the problem a matter of the reward system?

When we are particularly upset by a person's performance, it is easy to jump to conclusions and focus on the person. Make sure you gather your facts and think things through carefully before you schedule a session with the person.

The 7 Steps to Trust-Based Management

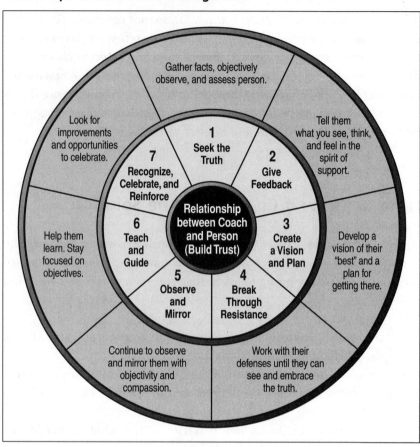

The 7 Steps to Trust-Based Management

A good manager is one who can work from both sides of the brain. We mentioned that coaching is about building a relationship, which is certainly a right-brain activity. Relationship building is not a linear process, it's not black and white, which is why some of us get frustrated in our relationships, particularly with employees. You cannot force or control a relationship. It is something that happens. Relationship building requires a different type of thinking and set of skills than building a product or system.

At the same time, we need to engage the other side of the brain. We need some structure, some process, a road map, if you will, for coaching people if we are going to be successful. There are certain principles that govern effective coaching, disciplines which must be in place, steps we must take if coaching is to produce the desired results. The relationship between you and the person is not the end. It is the primary means by which you are going to get the performance and growth you are seeking. The relationship is at the heart of the process but only part of it.

Shown at the left is The 7 Steps to Trust-Based Management process that when followed will help you build a trusting relationship *and* get the performance you are seeking. Each of the chapters that follow will explain in detail how to apply each step. As with any process, each step is connected to every other step. It's the application of these steps in an integrated, consistent fashion that makes the process work. If you fail to perform or perform ineffectively any one of the steps, it will significantly reduce the effectiveness of all your other coaching efforts.

What's Your Coaching Quotient?

If you wish to develop more of a coaching style of management, you need to know where you are on the continuum. Are you an old-style manager or an enlightened manager or somewhere in between? The whole coaching process is based on self-reflection and self-understanding which applies to you as well as the people you are leading. Here are some questions to help you determine how well you are coaching your people today.

1. Do you care as much about your people and their success as you do about your own?
   Yes ☐   No ☐

2. Do you focus as much on the people as you do on the work?
   Yes ☐   No ☐

3. Do you meet frequently with your people, individually and as a team, to reinforce the mission and goals and to give them feedback?
   Yes ☐   No ☐

4. When you meet with your people is it a dialogue? Do they talk as much or more than you do?
   Yes ☐   No ☐

5. When people "screw up," do you give them the benefit of the doubt, carefully gather the facts, and ask questions before rushing to judgment?
   Yes ☐   No ☐

6. When you are trying to get people to think or perform differently, do you take the time to ask questions of them so they can discover the idea on their own?
   Yes ☐   No ☐

7. When people perform exceptionally well are you truly happy for them and do you express how you feel to them?
   Yes ☐   No ☐

8. Do you involve people in the goal-setting and decision-making processes?
   Yes ☐   No ☐

9. Do you give people the right to disagree and have feelings without punishing them?
   Yes ☐   No ☐

10. Do you encourage people to speak their minds and challenge the system?
    Yes ☐   No ☐

11. Do you tell people the straight truth about their performance with compassion and understanding and do you hold them accountable?
    Yes ☐   No ☐

12. Do you resist the temptation to always tell people what you know and how you think they should do their jobs?
    Yes ☐   No ☐

13. Do you watch for the emotional content of your conversations with your people?
Yes ☐   No ☐

14. Do you admit to your people when you are wrong?
Yes ☐   No ☐

15. Do you spend as much time developing the excellent performers as you do the poor performers?
Yes ☐   No ☐

16. Do you stay focused on people's performance and refrain from letting your personal likes and dislikes interfere?
Yes ☐   No ☐

17. Do you stay constantly open to the idea that the way you see things may not be the way things are?
Yes ☐   No ☐

18. When you give feedback, is it immediate, meaning close to the time of the action or performance?
Yes ☐   No ☐

19. Do the majority of people thank you after you have given them feedback?
Yes ☐   No ☐

20. Would you like to have you as a manager?
Yes ☐   No ☐

Scoring: If you answered yes to 15 or more questions, you have already made the transition to a coaching style of management. Congratulations.

If you answered yes to 10 to 14 questions, you have adapted many of the coaching concepts but still have a way to go.

If you answered yes to fewer than 10 questions, you are still using old-style management methods. You may need to get yourself a coach!

PERSONAL APPLICATION CORNER

The Coach Approach to Home and Family Life

Most of us aren't too different at home than we are at work. We may be more reserved and professional but many of the same dynamics that occur between us and our peers, subordinates, and superiors are similar to those that go on between ourselves and our spouse or significant other, children, and parents.

Personal relationships, like work relationships, are also about power, ego, and self-esteem. The only difference is there is usually more at stake in our personal relationships. All too often in our home and family relationships we focus our efforts on getting our spouse and/or children to do the right thing—in other words, to do things our way. Sometimes in our efforts to get our children to be fine, upstanding, productive citizens, we break our relationship with them. We don't mean to but we do. And sometimes with our spouse or significant other we are so terrified of losing our own sense of individual power and control that we disempower the other person which ultimately hurts and sometimes destroys the relationship.

Something to Try: For one week, observe how you talk to and relate to your children and/or spouse or significant other (or any meaningful person in your life). Listen to the number of times you demand, judge, and criticize. Listen for the number of times you request, encourage, and affirm. For each of your family relationships, on a scale of 1 to 10, rate the quality of your relationship. What is the trust level? While you are observing, don't judge yourself or try to change the dynamic that is there (unless, of course, you have been really hurting the person).

At the end of the week, take some quiet time by yourself in a place where you can relax and you won't be disturbed. Reflect on the week, and for each of your family relationships, ask yourself how you would like the relationship to be. Be as descriptive as you can: what would it look like, how would it feel, what would you do differently, and how would they respond? Let those images be your goal as you work to develop more trusting relationships with the people who are most important to you.

CHAPTER TWO

The Relationship between Manager and Employee

The song "People" by Barbra Streisand always seemed a bit strange to us. For example, look at the line: "People. People who need people are the luckiest people in the world." Just who are those other people who don't need people? Aren't we all lucky? Can any of us get along in this world or achieve anything of importance without the help of others? Is there really such a thing as a self-made person?

And yet we are taught that to need something or someone is to display weakness. Rugged individualism is highly prized. Isn't that part of what our search for wealth and affluence is all about? The more affluence we have, the less we need or have to depend on others.

To be strong, independent, and self-reliant are certainly positive qualities, but like anything, when taken to extremes, they become our undoing. As humans we are made for each other. We have a built-in need to be in relationships with others. It's in our "hard drive." Unless we have a healthy interdependence with other people, our independence is compromised, our strength becomes our weakness, and our self-reliance leads us into isolation and alienation.

Maybe that's why so many of us are on Prozac today. Our affluence, technology, and lives lived at breakneck speed have separated us from one another. We feel empty because we've lost the human connection.

We've lost our sense of belonging, a sense of community. When we lose our human connections, we lose our juice. We become "human doings" without a healthy "Why?" behind our unending stream of activities. It is through other people that we learn about ourselves. It is through others that we are nurtured and sustained. It is through others that we are able to expand our view of the world. It is through and with others that we create meaning in life.

Healthy relationships are essential to a long, happy life; a rewarding, successful career; and a successful organization. Studies reveal that one of the shared characteristics of people who live to be 100 and beyond is that they have strong, nurturing relationships in their lives. The most successful leaders are those who are the most skilled at forging strong, trusting relationships. Constructive, productive relationships are the bedrock of every organization that wishes to be more than an overnight, short-lived success.

More Powerful than You Think

We look at leaders such as General Electric CEO Jack Welch and Microsoft founder Bill Gates and marvel at the impact they have on the lives of vast numbers of people, particularly the people who work for them. And yet, most of us serving as leaders, albeit on a less grand scale, completely miss the point. We, too, have an enormous impact on the lives of the people we are leading.

When you think about it, doesn't your boss have the capacity to make or break your day? If the boss speaks to you in a disparaging way on a given day, what kind of evening do you have? How is your spouse affected by your boss's behavior toward you? When the boss affirms you in some way or gives you a meaningful reward for your efforts, don't your spirits soar? Don't you feel more confident and willing to take risks?

We have seen bosses literally drive people to their graves and we have seen them change lives. We have seen them destroy careers and we have seen them lift people to heights of success and achievement which the individuals never dreamed possible. The individual, of course, ultimately determines the impact another person has on them, but the truth is bosses do have the capacity to dramatically influence people's lives.

You don't have to manage a $50 million budget or a staff of 500 to have an impact. You can be a first-line supervisor managing two or three people and make an enormous difference in a person's life. But first you must understand and believe how powerful and impactful you are in the ways you interact with your people.

▼OUR EXPERIENCE

The Meaning of Success

Once when I was coaching one of the top officers of a large company, I asked him how he defined success. *After thinking for a moment, he said for him it didn't have much to do with money; it had to do with having an impact, making a difference. By this definition he said he didn't feel he was very successful, despite the fact that he had a beautiful family, had a achieved a measure of wealth, and had risen to a high position within the company, managing over 230 people.*

This experience reminded me of how much we all want to make a difference and how little many of us know about how to do it. This particular person learned over time that it wasn't that difficult to be successful, to have an impact. He came to embrace the idea that it comes as a result of bringing a spirit of helpfulness to the people he was leading. The mantle of power came not from the formal authority bestowed on him by the company but from the followers themselves. He also learned that he had countless opportunities to impact his people and that, in fact, he was doing it every single day. He just didn't realize it.

—Bill

Built-in Barriers

Developing healthy relationships with the people you lead is no small feat. Boss-subordinate relationships can be especially complicated for the following reasons.

- There is a built-in imbalance of power by virtue of the fact that the boss has more formal authority.
- Many people carry with them a fair amount of baggage surrounding the boss which is why some people believe *boss* spells double-S-O-B backwards. People who have difficulty with authority figures

and/or who have suffered at the hands of poor bosses in the past often have difficulty seeing the boss objectively.
- There is so much on the line: the boss's success is dependent upon her people's performance, and each person's livelihood, to a large degree, is at the mercy of the boss.

Understanding and managing these complexities is a big part of a manager's job.

A relationship is what happens between two people when they each bring their own unique set of hopes, fears, expectations, motives, complexes, personality traits, experiences, and interpersonal skills to the interaction. A dynamic is created which is both conscious and unconscious. Obviously, the more aware the two people are of the dynamics of the relationship, the better they can work to improve it. The dynamic that exists between two people results in their experience of the relationship—sometimes positive, sometimes negative.

Many of us have this idea that relationships should be easy. When relationships work, we hardly think about what's making them work. But when they become troublesome, our best efforts to understand the relationships and get them back on track often fail. What works in one relationship won't work in another. Every relationship is unique and has a certain mystery to it. Relationships take time and some take more time than others.

It's hard to pinpoint exactly what makes some relationships blossom and grow and others never quite make it. If you've ever tried to rebuild a failing relationship, you know what we mean. Perhaps that's what makes relationships so interesting and so challenging. We can't force them, we can't control them, and we can never fully understand them. The best we an do is be fully present for them, allow them to develop in their own time, and do our part in developing and nurturing them.

Characteristics of a Healthy Relationship

While we can never fully understand why some professional relationships work and some don't, there are some characteristics which we know are fundamental to a healthy working relationship. Here's what must be there if you are going to have a successful relationship with each person you are leading.

- *It is built on an even playing field.* People must view one another as equally important to the relationship. It is understood that the boss has more formal authority, but in a healthy boss-subordinate relationship, it's more like a partnership. There's a mutual respect. The manager never abuses his power and never reminds people of it. In fact, the manager works hard at making people feel that their ideas and contributions are as important as his.

- *Needs are communicated and honored.* Every relationship is about getting needs met. That's one of the reasons we enter relationships to begin with. The problem occurs when one person gets hurt |and angry because a need she expected the other person to meet doesn't get met. The real problem too often is that the other person never knew about the need or expectation in the first place. In every healthy relationship, people are allowed to have needs and they take responsibility for communicating their needs in a timely, constructive manner. Each person works to meet her own needs, the needs of the other person, and the needs of the relationship—which, by the way, is quite an art and too seldom practiced by people in relationships.

- *Time and attention is given.* Some relationships take more care and feeding than others but no relationship can grow and survive unless there is time spent together. And when time is spent, the two people must give one another their complete attention—something that is hard to do when people, projects, and tasks are pulling you in a thousand directions. It's not easy to find the time but it is essential. You can't be multitasked when you are coaching. You won't be present and the person will know it. A lot of us out there are starved for some real attention—the kind of attention where we know we've been seen, heard, and understood. Attention is Miracle-Gro for relationships. Without it they whither and die.

▼OUR EXPERIENCE

The Secretary Who Was Always Late

Early in my career as a manager, I had a secretary named Amy who insisted on being 10 to 15 minutes late every morning. In my position, I was serving a lot of internal customers so it was important that she be on time. Her lateness seemed to be out of character for Amy because she was an excellent performer otherwise. She had excellent skills and worked hard when she was there. She never refused to work late if we were working against a tight deadline. For some reason though, she was always late.

At the time, I was working very long hours (before I learned the meaning of the word *balance*). I had a lot of responsibilities and a fair amount of pressure at a very young age. Every morning I would whiz by Amy's desk as I made a beeline for my office and would quickly mutter without making eye contact, "Hi, Amy. How are you?" It was obviously not a question and barely a greeting.

After coaching Amy repeatedly about her tardiness, we decided we would part company but not before a colleague of mine shared with me the real reason Amy was late. She said she was late because I never paid her much attention, never asked her how her weekend was. She felt ignored. I was so focused on the work I had before me each day that I forgot the people who were supporting me in accomplishing the work. Amy and I had very little basis for a relationship because I gave her so little attention. Had I known her better I would have been able to sense what was bothering her or she would have trusted me enough to tell me. Because there was no trust, there was no basis for a behavior change. It was a powerful learning experience for me.

—Diane

- *People feel safe with each other.* Isn't that what we are all looking for—some safe haven where, for a few minutes anyway, when we are in the presence of another human being, we can let our guard down? We don't have to be constantly looking over our shoulders because we know the other person has our best interests at heart. Emotional and psychological safety is what we get when there is trust between two people. The moment people create that safe place, they have set the stage for amazing things to happen.

- *Differences are accepted and respected.* Each person is free to be himself. He expresses his thoughts, ideas, and feelings even though they may be different from the other person. Healthy relationships usually aren't free of disagreement or conflict. If we always agree, there is no stimulus to get out of ourselves and see things differently. The key is that when differences arise, we don't judge, criticize, and reject the other person for the difference and we don't discuss them with other people.

Getting Yourself Out of the Way

We spoke earlier about the power managers have to change lives. The truth is, you can't save or change anyone but yourself. You can work to set up an environment which can foster a person's growth and development but you don't have control over it. You can't make it happen. The power to change lies within the person. The relationship is the catalyst.

The minute you think you have people figured out or that you have their answers or that you are going to be their savior or the person to turn them into a champion, you are on dangerous ground. When your own ego gets in the driver's seat of the relationship, watch out. The process is now about you instead of them. Your job is to be the facilitator of the process, not the director of their destiny.

To be a good manager you need the right blend of confidence and humility. The confidence comes from knowing you've got some good stuff to share with your people—knowledge, insights, experiences, etc. The humility comes from knowing that human beings are too complex, too magnificent, too unpredictable to be grasped by the mind of another human being. The best managers are those that know the wisdom of honoring their "I don't knows."

The coaching process is an ongoing journey in which the manager and employee are constantly asking the right questions—questions that will lead to a better understanding of the person: her strengths and weaknesses, her opportunities for growth, her hopes and fears, her motives; all of the factors that affect the person's ability to perform and reach more of her potential in the context of the job. As a manager you are merely a guide on the person's journey to self-discovery.

There will be times when you are so sure you have the answer and the temptation to tell the other person so will be strong. It will take everything in you to keep your mouth shut. There will be times when it is appropriate to suggest or recommend. As the person's supervisor you will delegate tasks and communicate expectations which will take the form of telling. In times of crisis you may need to direct people with no questions asked. When you are trying to help people grow in a certain direction and discover something new about themselves, the best you can do is ask questions, share your own experience, tell stories. Your job is to light the fire of imagination which is where all new thinking and ideas come from.

When a person achieves something of significance or has a breakthrough of some kind as a result of your work together, do not take credit—give it all back to the person. It is natural to want to take some of the glory but it's counterproductive to the person's growth and the relationship. Your fascination should be with the process—not yourself. Instead of saying to yourself, "Wow! What a great manager I am. He couldn't have done it without me." Think instead, "Wow! This process is amazing and so is this person. I don't know exactly how the change came about but I am fortunate to have witnessed it." The more you celebrate *their* successes, the more they will thank you for it.

Defining Responsibilities

One of the misperceptions many people have when they are in a relationship which isn't a relationship of equals, such as a parent-child or boss-subordinate relationship, is that the person with the formal authority is responsible for the relationship. If either party subscribes to this belief, an unhealthy dependence is set up and the relationship is in trouble. From the outset, there should be a clear understanding of who is responsible for what.

On an individual basis, you and your employees will want to have some dialogue about the expectations you have of one another. Here are some suggested guidelines.

Responsibilities of the Manager

- To help the person develop clearly defined performance and development objectives and stay focused on them
- To clearly communicate her expectations of the person and ensure that she understands them
- To meet the work needs of the person (resources, information, feedback, recognition, etc.) so that the person can meet the needs of the job
- To give frequent constructive feedback (not just once or twice a year at review time) on how well the person is meeting the objectives on an ongoing basis
- To hold the person accountable for his behavior and performance
- To help the person see what she can or cannot see about herself

- To listen openly to the person so that the manager can understand the person's thinking, actions, and feelings
- To provide the training and development necessary for the person's growth

Responsibilities of the Employee

- To be committed to his own developmental process
- To ask for clarification if she doesn't understand her responsibilities
- To be open to receiving constructive feedback even though it may sometimes be difficult to hear
- To give honest, frequent feedback to the manager on a timely basis
- To constructively disagree and not cave in to the manager's way of seeing things when it is something the person feels strongly about
- To communicate to the manager when his work needs are not being met
- To follow through on action steps agreed upon with the manager

These are just a sampling of some of the responsibilities of manager and employee. Defining your responsibilities and expectations of each other can help enormously to minimize disappointments and misunderstandings.

Honoring Boundaries

Healthy boundaries are intrinsic to healthy relationships. So what exactly is a boundary? Boundaries are the lines drawn between two people which protect the integrity and privacy of the individuals in the relationship. Even in the most intimate, personal relationships, boundaries are essential. In fact, without healthy boundaries, intimacy is impossible. Intimacy without boundaries becomes merging. When people merge emotionally and psychologically they lose themselves and eventually split from the relationship. While we are all made to be in relationships with others, we are also made to be separate, intact individuals with a strong sense of *I*.

Workplace intimacy is different from what we normally think of as intimacy. (No, we are not talking about office romances.) When we talk about workplace intimacy we are referring to a genuine human connection between two people which is based on mutual respect and regard. We are referring to a relationship in which the two people feel accepted and appreciated for who they are. There is a feeling of safety.

At the same time, the relationship should not be too personal—sometimes a fine line to walk. The primary focus of the relationship should be the work. Periodically, your conversation might venture into the realm of the personal which is actually good for the relationship because it makes each person more human. It should, however, be kept to a minimum and it should not be information or conversation which is of a highly personal nature. Telling a person, for example, that you went to a movie the night before is acceptable but telling her the details of your date is not.

A healthy distance between manager and employee is important to the relationship. The old saying "familiarity breeds contempt" is particularly true at work. At the same time, however, we all know of relationships between boss and employee that are very familiar and they work. Maybe somewhere in your own career you have had a relationship with a boss in which the two of you had a real affinity for one another. You knew a lot about one another. Maybe the person even changed the course of your life and career.

There are no hard and fast rules when it comes to relationships but when relationships become too personal at work, it can be difficult for people to remain objective. A manager's first priority is to act in the best interest of the team and the organization. If he becomes too involved in the personal life of one of the team members, it can compromise the manager's ability to act in the best interest of the team and organization.

When people are too revealing, too vulnerable with one another at work, they often live to regret it. There is a fear that the information can be used against them and sometimes it is. When one person is drawn into the personal problems of another, the focus can easily become the person's problems instead of the work. Work should not be a place for people to process their personal problems. In fact, keeping work and personal problems separate can actually help people. Work can provide them with some temporary relief when they leave their problems at the door when coming to work.

People may from time to time reveal something of a personal nature—something they would not want going over the company voice mail—but those times should be the exception and there should be a work-related reason for sharing the information. Here are some general guidelines for the types of boundaries you will want to honor and require that they be honored for you.

- *Values.* What a person values in his life is very personal. It is never our place to tell another person that his values are wrong. If the person's work values don't match with the company's values and it is affecting the work, then that is another story. Just don't expect people to care about the same things you do.
- *Time and space.* This goes both ways. The manager needs to have a healthy respect for the employee's time and space. If the manager, for example, has set a time for a meeting with the person and keeps her waiting outside his office for 30 minutes, that is a violation of the person's boundary. The employee should also respect the manager's time and space. She, for example, should not barge into the manager's office uninvited and interrupt what the manager is doing.
- *Limits.* Everyone has limitations—the places beyond which people cannot go without doing damage to themselves. It's up to the person to determine what those limitations are, not the manager. As a manager, there will be times when you must push a person to achieve more than he thinks he can achieve, but be careful not to push him too hard or ask for too much. If he starts to appear confused, too anxious, or afraid, back off.
- *Confidentiality.* Nothing will destroy trust faster than revealing to someone else what someone told you in confidence. If the person didn't tell you not to keep the information confidential and you have any doubt that the person could be upset, check with the person first.
- *Personal information.* "Don't ask, don't tell" is a good motto for keeping work relationships businesslike. Don't ask a person questions that are too personal, and if the person reveals information that is personal in nature, tell her you would rather not hear it because it is not appropriate in a work relationship.

It's not enough to know what your own boundaries are. You must communicate them to your people—particularly the boundaries concerning time and space. Some of them don't need to be openly discussed. You simply need to model them in such a way that others get the message.

More than Your Words

Good leaders are experts at communicating in all its forms. We were reminded some time ago of the power of nonverbal communication when we attended a meeting at a $20 billion company. The meeting was with the CEO and his direct reports. As each of the reports spoke and presented, the wise CEO spoke little but continuously encouraged and supported them through the nod of his head, the wink of an eye, an open body posture, and facial expressions signaling approval. With each small gesture, and there were many, we could see the confidence and energy of the individuals and the team rise.

In any relationship, of course, communication is taking place on a number of different levels—many of which are unconscious. We place so much emphasis on the words that we speak and very little on the other aspects of our communication which often communicate far more loudly than our words.

As you know, words are cheap and too freely spoken by most of us. If you want your words to have power and impact you must make sure that they line up with what you really think and believe, what you feel, and what you do. That's how you build trust.

When we say one thing but feel or think another, we set people up for confusion. When communication is not clear, people spin their own stories about what you really meant, who you really are, what your real motives are, etc.

This doesn't mean that you say everything that crosses your mind or that you act on your feelings. It does mean you stay aware of what your real thoughts and feelings are. It means you pay attention to what your body may be communicating through your facial expressions, body tension, hand gestures, and eye contact.

Our emotions are powerful and are carried in the body. If you aren't careful, your body can easily communicate one message while your words communicate another. A good rule of thumb is to assume that people can read your mind and feelings. This is not always true but they are always picking up clues as to what is really going on with you. Your job is to manage the clues so that you are able to communicate the message you want. We are not talking about manipulating people or your communication. We are talking about being honest and congruent in what you say, think, and do.

Relationship Traps

Have you ever had a relationship that was humming along just fine when all of a sudden it fell apart? Or maybe from the beginning the relationship just never did quite work. Well, it is probably because the relationship fell into a trap. Here are just some of the traps you will want to watch for.

- *Role playing.* When people play roles, they aren't being themselves and when they are not being themselves, there cannot be intimacy or real human connection. Role playing is about hiding. In a husband-wife relationship, for example, one person might play the role of the strong, invincible one and the other the role of the weak, helpless one. In a boss-subordinate relationship, the manager could play the role of the all-knowing one and the employee the naïve, passive one.
- *Stereotyping.* We like to figure things and people out because it gives us an illusion of safety and predictability. If you label a person a certain way and decide that he is this or that kind of person, you will limit the growth and development of the person and of the relationship. Your beliefs and assumptions will erect automatic barriers to discovering anything new about the person.
- *Conflict avoidance.* When we care about another person and a relationship we often don't want to do or say anything to upset the good feelings that each person has come to enjoy. Conflicts arising from differences of opinion and misunderstandings are inevitable and if you don't deal with them as they arise, the relationship will eventually deteriorate. Resolving conflicts as they occur is the way you keep the air clean. Clean air is a must for healthy relationships.
- *Neglect.* Once you have reached a quality of relationship that is comfortable, it's only the beginning. You have got to keep riding your relationship bicycle. You must keep doing the things that fostered the growth and development of the relationship in the beginning: spending time, getting to know one another, affirming one another, sharing thoughts and ideas, learning together, working together, and respecting one another. More relationships fail from neglect than probably anything else.

- *Comparison.* Every relationship is unique and to compare it to other relationships doesn't get you very far. Besides, no one really knows what goes on between two people. Appearances can be very deceiving. Just keep focusing on making your relationship better instead of focusing on what other relationships seem to have that yours doesn't.
- *Projecting.* Sometimes we need people to be something or be a certain way for our own purposes—usually so we can feel better about ourselves. If we don't have a particularly high sense of self-esteem, we may, for example, project our own negative qualities onto the other person so we can't see the person clearly for who she is. Our perception of her is distorted by our own stuff. Or a person, for example, may have a need for the manager to be bigger than life, to be his hero, so he projects all kinds of qualities onto the manager which doesn't allow the manager to be herself.

These are just some of the traps to watch out for in your relationships with people at work, as well as your personal relationships. When either of you fall into one or more of these traps, the first thing you need to do is acknowledge it. Often, that's all it takes to get back on track.

How to Start a Coaching Relationship

We coach a lot of executives starting new jobs as a way of helping them acclimate themselves quickly to the new culture and their responsibilities. One of our frequent challenges is getting the person's boss excited about the person joining the company. Most of the time bosses see a new person as work. They have to take valuable time telling the person where to find things, how to access information, who to go to for what, etc. They see it as a chore.

When we coach a newly hired executive, we work with the person's boss as well and without fail the boss comments on what a joy it was having us help orient the new person to the job and the company. When we asked one boss why, he said at our suggestion he gave the person far more feedback than he normally would have and it made all the difference. The person responded very favorably which got the relationship off to a good start.

If you hire a new person, you have a clean slate with the person. From day one you can and should apply The 7 Steps to Trust-Based Management process which we will begin discussing in the next chapter. Starting anew with someone you've been managing for a while is another story. What do you do? Do you announce to your staff or to a person that you are no longer going to be his manager, but instead his coach? We don't think so.

One of the first things you will want to do is an assessment of your current relationship. Never assume that you know how the people who report to you feel about you or the condition of your relationship with them. Employees are very good at presenting a face that differs from their true feelings as a way of protecting themselves. Many managers are shocked to find out what their people really feel about them. What you see is not always what is real. Sometimes you may be pleasantly surprised.

You are going to have to meet people where they are and slowly begin to build a new kind of relationship if you haven't coached them in the past. The key issue is trust. Do people trust you to tell them the truth? Do you trust them? Do they trust that you care about them as people and not just as a means of getting the job done? Do people know what to expect from you? These are just some of the things you will want to find out as you assess your relationship. This information can be invaluable to you.

There are a number of ways you can find out how people feel. You can have one-on-one meetings. If you do, you will have to work especially hard to convince them that you really do want the truth and that there will be absolutely no repercussions or retaliations for telling the truth. (You, of course, must be prepared to hear some things you don't want to hear.) You must hear what they say without defending or judging. If you don't, you will silence them. Never shoot the messenger if you want the truth.

Another way is to ask your human resources department or an outside consultant to do one-on-one interviews with your people. This is one of the best ways to get the straight story. Again, people must be assured that their confidences will be maintained and that nothing they say will be used against them in any way.

You can also ask people to complete anonymous questionnaires. You can administer them yourself, or to ensure greater confidentiality, you can ask your human resources department to distribute them and report the results back to you.

Once you complete your assessment you will have a better idea of how far you will have to go to build a true coaching relationship. Periodically, you will want to stop and evaluate the relationship using similar tools. Hopefully, you will have built enough trust that people will be willing to speak candidly with you about how they feel.

What You Need to Know

Former New York mayor Ed Koch used to ask, "How am I doing?" Here's a questionnaire to help you evaluate yourself and your relationships with your people. With some rewording of the questions you can use it to find out how your people feel. If the questionnaire is the basis of personal interviews, it would be better to have an objective, third party conduct the interviews. If you present it in writing, you will want to give it to a number of people to protect the anonymity of the individuals.

1. Do I clearly define and communicate my expectations of people?
   Yes ☐   No ☐

2. When I coach people, do I remain objective and focus on the behavior and performance?
   Yes ☐   No ☐

3. Do I follow through on my commitments to people?
   Yes ☐   No ☐

4. Am I consistent in what I say and do? Do I walk the talk?
   Yes ☐   No ☐

5. Do I refrain from showing favoritism and treat everyone equally?
   Yes ☐   No ☐

6. Do I encourage people to take risks? Do I stand up for them?
   Yes ☐   No ☐

7. Do I keep people informed about important matters?
   Yes ☐   No ☐

8. Do I allow and encourage people to speak their minds and disagree?
   Yes ☐   No ☐

9. Am I careful to always give people credit for their accomplishments? Do I refrain from stealing the spotlight from them?
   Yes ☐   No ☐

10. Do I tell people the truth and give them constructive feedback on a regular basis?
    Yes ☐   No ☐

11. Do I care about the interests and concerns of my people? Do I demonstrate it to them?
    Yes ☐   No ☐

12. Am I competent in my job? Do people see me as competent?
    Yes ☐   No ☐

13. Do I treat people as an equal partner?
    Yes ☐   No ☐

14. Do I give people freedom and trust that they will perform unless I have reason to believe otherwise?
    Yes ☐   No ☐

15. Do I believe that most people are well intentioned and want to do a good job?
    Yes ☐   No ☐

Scoring: If you answered yes to 13 or more questions, your relationship with others should be solid. There should be a healthy trust and respect between you and your people.

If you answered yes to 9 to 12 questions, you have some work to do but you have some trust to build upon.

If you answered yes to fewer than 9 questions, you have a lot of work to do. One of your first jobs will be to regain their trust.

PERSONAL APPLICATION CORNER

Think back to the personal relationships you observed and reflected on in Chapter 1. Take one of those relationships and make it your personal mission to improve the quality of the relationship by building some bridges of trust. Here are ten questions to think about:

1. Do I expect too much of the other person?
2. Do I honor the person's boundaries and do I set healthy boundaries for myself?
3. Have we ever sat down and calmly discussed how we feel about the relationship?
4. Am I guilty of labeling and stereotyping the person?
5. Do I expect the person to screw up or do I look for the positive in the person?
6. Do I give the person freedom to be her own unique person or do I need her to be a certain way for my own benefit?
7. Do I discuss problems in the relationship as they occur or do I hold on to them and explode later?
8. Do I keep his confidence and refrain from using sensitive information against him?
9. Do I spend time with her?
10. Does the person know I am 100 percent for him?

Something to Try: Most of the time when people don't get along, they are afraid the other person is going to hurt them in some way—or will continue hurting them. The arguing and anger are simply defenses for staying safe. For one week, try to do the following with the person you selected:

- Do not criticize, blame, or judge—even if something she does sends you through the roof.
- Sincerely affirm him at least two to three times during the week or whenever you can.
- Find some way to let her know that you truly care about her and wish to have a better relationship.

Taking these steps will not solve all the problems of the relationship but they will help to create a more safe place so that you can begin to understand one another better and strengthen the relationship.

CHAPTER THREE

STEP 1

Seek the Truth

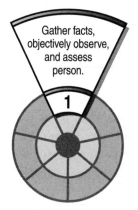

Gather facts, objectively observe, and assess person.

When you get to know your people and observe their performance, you empower yourself to give them the kind of feedback which improves performance and builds trust.

There is a quote from the Bible which says, "You shall know the truth and the truth shall set you free." That's what coaching is all about— helping people discover and embrace the truth about themselves, warts and all, so that they can change and grow. Too many people stay stuck and static in their personal and professional growth, repeating the same old patterns, because they have a distorted view of who they are, and in the case of work, how they are performing. Unless people have a realistic view of who they are, including their strengths and weaknesses, they can't move to a new place. It's like trying to get to San Francisco from Chicago when your real starting point is New York.

Seeking the truth is the first step in The 7 Steps to Trust-Based Management process. When we talk about seeking the truth about someone, we are talking about getting to know him as a person. It's the information you need to know in order to effectively lead the person to his best performance. Seeking the truth also means objectively observing a person's performance and assessing it fairly. Understanding him as a person provides you with a backdrop, a context for observing his performance. It can give you insight into why a person might be performing in a particular manner. Seeking the truth or the facts about a person's performance is the hard data you need to effectively coach a person. Whenever you are seeking information, your most powerful tool, of course, is always the question.

That reminds us of an executive we were once asked to coach who thought he always had to have the answers. In all the times we observed him interacting with his people, never once did we see him ask any of them a question. He constantly issued declaratives such as: "Don't tell me those things. I'll tell you the real answer" and "You don't know what you are talking about. I'll tell you what you are going to do."

Through coaching we found that the man was actually insecure and thought he had to have all the answers. He thought that's what leadership was all about. He confessed that when people did tell him what was going on, matters got even worse. He thought he had to have even more answers so he purposely tried to restrict people from putting him on the spot. In many ways, the man was quite brilliant but he was inept as a manager of people.

The result of this style of management was that he was never working from the real facts and he had the highest rate of turnover of any division in the company. In fact, the feedback from the 360-degree interviews was so negative that executive management thought they would have to terminate him soon. Surprisingly, he responded very quickly to the coaching and made major changes in his management style. Most important, he stopped barking and dictating and started asking questions. This story should be reassuring to all of us. If you are an old dog you can still learn new tricks.

Why the Truth Is Hard to Come by

Everything rests on getting as true a picture of a person and her performance as possible. If you miss this step, forget about developing a relationship based on trust. Getting a true picture of a person and her performance is not as easy as it may seem for the following reasons:

- The picture can be distorted by your own lens—the way you see the world based on your own unique background, history, and experiences.
- Some people are more complex than others and harder to understand.
- People always put their best foot forward when dealing with the boss.

- Factors can interfere with our perception of how well a person is performing, such as the culture, lack of resources, and faulty systems.
- People are constantly changing and cannot be pegged.
- Much of a person's performance and behavior is out of the view of the manager.
- Unfortunately, some people outright lie to themselves and to others.

Establishing the Basis for Observation

Nothing annoys people more than to receive feedback that is off base, irrelevant, and unjustified. One of the most common causes of such reactions is the failure of the manager to clearly define and communicate the job responsibilities, the standards the person is expected to meet, and the job objectives from the beginning. When people have only a vague idea of what they are supposed to do, we set them up for failure. They end up working in what we call the pain of ambiguity. They spend most of their time and energy second guessing the boss and trying to understand what he wants. Because of the fear associated with such ambiguity, they work in a protective mode instead of a productive mode. They spend more of their time trying to avoid being caught blindsided than they do concentrating on how they can perform the job better.

We saw a classic example of this once when we were working with a newly hired executive. The company had asked us to help him adapt to the new environment and the position. The individual was very quiet and laid back and hesitant to engage with others. He was viewed as being extremely powerful because of the vast amount of knowledge and information he had, but he didn't share it with anyone. He played everything very close to the vest.

As a result of his management style, his people were constantly trying to second guess him. His entire division was in a state of frozen animation and nothing was getting done. Through coaching he told us he was giving them time to adjust to him and giving himself time to understand the culture. In today's world, of course, leaders must be able to adjust quickly and cannot afford to leave their people in a state of limbo. We also learned from him that he wasn't mistrustful of others. He was in fact shy and not particularly comfortable with people. The motivation behind people's behavior is often not what we think it is.

Nevertheless, he quickly learned to fill the information vacuum he had created for his people and began acting as a true leader.

The clearer you are about your expectations, the better performance you are going to receive. Don't tell someone something once and expect her to get it. Expectations should be in writing and referred to on a consistent basis. It is said that if you want someone to remember something, you must tell him seven times. On a day-to-day basis, people are bombarded with information, much of it meaningless. You have to compete for their attention. Most people are fairly task oriented which often doesn't lead to the accomplishment of objectives. Your job is to keep them focused. It works the same way as when you put a magnifying glass on a piece of paper with the sun's rays focused on it; it burns because there is a concentration of energy. Clearly defined expectations allow them to focus their energies in the right direction.

Getting to Know Your People

Have you ever worked with a person for a long time and still not known much about her? All you know is the carefully crafted persona she presents to you. Maybe you've just never taken the time. Perhaps you are so focused on the work and getting the job done that spending time talking about anything other than work seems nonproductive. Whatever the reason, it is vitally important that you know and understand your people as individuals. At the same time, of course, you don't want to become too personal. You want to maintain that fine line—a certain amount of detachment which is sometimes very difficult to do.

What does it mean to know your people? Here are just some of the things you should know about people if you are going to be able to motivate them and coach them effectively.

- What do they care about and what they don't care about?
- What gets them excited at work?
- How do they perform under pressure?
- How sensitive are they? How well do they take criticism?
- What are their past work experiences and accomplishments?
- What kind of team players are they?
- What are their career goals?
- How assertive are they?

- How much insight do they have into themselves?
- What is the gap between their real strengths and weaknesses and what they think they are?
- How willing are they to speak their minds?
- How well organized are they?

The only way you can find the answers to these questions is by spending time with them. Every time we mention the importance of spending time we are sure it is met with a sigh of frustration. What manager has time for that today? Everywhere we go people tell us that they are being asked to do twice the amount of work with half the amount of resources.

Think about this: The most successful business leader and CEO of our time, Jack Welch of General Electric, says that we cannot cut costs on talent. As he puts it, "You've got to build it." If Jack Welch spends the majority of his time on people issues, what causes us to believe that lower-level managers can afford to spend any less? Yes, it is time consuming but the payoff is big.

We once coached a person who appeared to be a real loner. She never tried to draw people out and she never offered the smallest piece of information about her personal life to the point that people wondered if she had one. To most people she was a real enigma. As we coached her, she shared with us that she thought she should be strictly business—to be anything else, in her mind, was unprofessional. What she didn't realize was that by relating to her people in such an impersonal way, she had no common ground from which to work. Getting the work accomplished was a real struggle because she had no personal connection with her people.

Sometimes you can learn a lot about a person by talking about things that are not work related: what are his hobbies, did he see a particular movie and what did he think of it, what did he think of something that appeared in the news. The key is to draw him out so you can understand better how he thinks and what motivates him.

Some people have narrower boundaries than others, meaning they are comfortable revealing very little about themselves. Those boundaries should be honored. Others have very loose boundaries, sometimes too loose, in which case you will have to watch the kinds of questions you ask them. One question could open up a stream of information which reveals too much and is too personal. You must learn the skill of politely cutting people off when the conversation goes too far. We've all been there.

The point is, you've got to pay attention. Not just with your head but also with your heart. You need to rely on your intuitive side as well as your rational side in getting to know people. The key is to see them as human beings with needs, hopes, fears, and idiosyncrasies—not just a means to getting the job done. If they don't feel you care about them as people, it will be impossible for you to coach them effectively.

Too Quick to Judge

Studies show that most people make up their minds about a person in the first 30 seconds of meeting her. Now that's a scary thought. To think we could take in, appreciate, and understand another human being in such a short period of time doesn't give any of us much of a chance to be seen for who we are.

In fact, it has been proven that in those first 30 seconds when someone meets a new person he makes the following five decisions:

1. Do I trust the person?
2. Am I attracted to the person?
3. Do I think the person is smart and intelligent?
4. Do I have something in common with the person?
5. Do I want to see the person again?

Judging people and their behavior too quickly and too severely is probably one of the major obstacles to people forming healthy relationships. Here are some of the results that occur when we judge the people we are managing too quickly.

- We look for behavior and performance that will justify our preconceived idea of the person.
- We unconsciously transmit our judgments of the person to him, which erodes trust.
- Everything we observe about the person is colored by our judgment.
- We take actions based on our prejudgments, which are unfair.
- People feel they don't have a chance because you have already made up your mind.

- We see them in absolutes and make sweeping generalizations about them.
- Our judgments keep us from getting to know the person better.
- People see us as a poor leader because we manage according to personalities.

Prejudging can be very costly in the workplace. Once we had been asked to assess the final candidates for an executive position the company was trying to fill. When we presented our findings to the human resource professional, she became quite angry and indignant when our data from the tests conflicted with her assessment of one individual. She said, "I don't care what your tests show. I can tell you in a nanosecond that this guy is an idiot and is incapable of performing in this company." Interestingly, she came to this conclusion after a three to four minute conversation. The empirically sound tests we gave the candidate showed that the person was off the charts in intelligence, decision-making ability, and cognitive skills, but nothing could change the human resource representative's mind. The candidate, of course, would not have reported to the human resource person but she kept him from getting the job.

The candidate remained at the company he was with which was a direct competitor of the company at which he was being considered for employment. Over the years his career soared and some people in the executive ranks of the company that had passed him by said later that the decision not to hire him had been a costly one and had actually hurt their company. All because one person was too quick to judge.

As we said in Chapter 2, to be a good manager you have to be able to get yourself out of the way. You've got to have a clear screen. How many times have you disliked a person you were managing because some of her personality traits just rubbed you the wrong way? Or maybe you didn't like the way she looked. Or maybe she was from a different ethnic group which you knew little about. Can you honestly say you didn't let any of your likes and dislikes affect your objectivity when evaluating her performance?

You may be saying to yourself, all right, you made the point. But it can't be made enough. More problems are caused in the workplace by managers who can't be objective and who allow themselves the luxury of acting out their prejudices on others than by anything else. The question is: "Do you want to be comfortable or do you want to be successful?" If you expect to like and be comfortable with every person who works for you, you are shooting yourself in the foot. There are a lot of talented, gifted people out there who we may not choose as friends but who can do a terrific job for us, provided we get ourselves out of the way and treat them fairly.

OUR EXPERIENCE

To Look Again

Some time ago my husband and I went to the Harley-Davidson dealership where we purchased our motorcycle. My husband and I were making our periodic trip to the store—something we do on a fairly regular basis for reasons which I'm not totally clear; I think it has something to do with adjusting his testosterone levels and pampering the closet rebel that lives inside his conservative soul.

As we drove into the parking lot, we saw through the lenses of our Ray-Ban glasses a rather strange looking couple dismount their iron horses and enter the store. Dressed in black leathers with a bandanna tied around his head of shoulder length hair, the man was a scary looking dude. The woman was a tiny little thing lost in her clothes. Her jeans were about four sizes too big and when she took off her helmet she replaced it with a baseball cap which she put on backward.

The image before us prompted a small but assured voice within one of the canyons of my mind: "Those people are not our kind of people." While my husband talked Harley talk to the shop owner, I took a small step out of my box to strike up a conversation with those people. Much to the surprise of my sometimes narrow view, those people, Roy and Milicete, were artists—he a sculptor in New York City and she a classical guitarist. What shocked us even more was that they had a kind of unspoiled innocence about them. And they had some very valuable information about motorcycling that we had been seeking for quite some time.

If we were to sum up all the talk about diversity in one word, it would be respect. *The term respect comes from the Latin word* respicere, *which means the willingness to look again. When we are willing to take a second look, we show respect for ourselves and for those we are looking at. When we take a second look, we give up our fixed view of a person or situation so that we can receive from him. When we look again, we allow people to be who they are instead of what we need or want them to be.*

—Diane

Sources of Information

Remember, your job is to get as accurate and comprehensive a picture of a person as possible. As you gather information about her performance, you will also be gathering information which will help you understand the person better. There are three primary sources for gathering the information you need to effectively coach people: 1) your own direct observation, 2) the perceptions of others, and 3) formal assessment tools.

Overreliance on any one of these sources can keep you from getting a complete picture. What you are seeking is a gestalt of the person and his work. Your own observation is not enough. The person may present one face to you and a totally different face to others within the organization with whom he interfaces. If you base your evaluation too heavily on what others say, you may miss something. Other people may not be objective and the sampling of people you speak with may not be representative of how the majority feels. Assessment tools can be very valuable but are only as good as the person who is evaluating the test. Assessments provide no magic answer and are dangerous when used alone and out of context.

Observing with the Eye of an Eagle

You'll want to constantly keep one eye on them and one eye on the work. Your observations should be constant—not just around review time. We aren't talking about policing people or standing over their shoulders, but taking a genuine interest in their work and how they perform their work. The more interest you take in them, the more they will reveal to you. Your job is to constantly look for ways you can be helpful to them.

The trendy term *management by walking around* is nothing more than an attempt to get managers up and out of their offices so they can learn what is really going on; so they can observe first hand. As you know, the boss is very often the last to know, so you can't rely solely on what others tell you. Most people are predisposed to telling the boss what she wants to hear which is often a far cry from the truth. You have to develop your observation skills—almost like a detective. Not that you are trying to spy on people or catch them doing something wrong—which reminds us of another trendy management theme, *catch them doing some-*

thing right. You can't catch them doing something right unless you are out in the ranks observing.

Your skills of observation should also be used in combination with your intuitive skills. Pay attention to the little voice in your head that whispers to you from time to time: "Something doesn't seem right here. I wonder what's really going on." That's the time to get out among them and find out the truth. Don't expect to get the truth by asking the direct question. Most of the time you have to come in the back door and piece the information together to get the picture. In addition to finding out specific information about a person's performance, you are learning about the context in which he is working.

We had a client once who was extremely skilled at observation and getting to know his people. He was the CEO of a highly successful company. He was a taskmaster who had extremely high standards and the 500 people who worked at the headquarters office knew it. He also had a wonderful sense of humor and used it to make people feel special.

Almost every day he would take a walk through the headquarters office, chatting and kidding with people, one-on-one. His kidding was usually about something personal (not inappropriately so) that he knew about the person. It could be something as innocuous as a loud tie the person was wearing that day or a haircut she had gotten recently. He would joke with the person and occasionally ask him something about his work. The result was that each person felt special because the CEO knew something about her. He took the time to acknowledge each one as a person. He was interested in each individual's work. In the course of his daily walks, he learned a lot about the people *and* the work. Most of the time, people never even knew what valuable pieces of information he was gleaning.

Characteristics of Good Observers

The manner in which you observe, must of course fit with your own individual style. Observing without being invasive is an art. It has to do with the spirit or motivation behind your observing and your skill at getting at the information you are seeking. People can sense when you are genuinely interested in them and their work and when you are trying to build a case against them. Here are some of the characteristics of good observers.

- They keep their eyes and ears open at all times.
- They watch for small nuances (e.g., body language, facial expressions, etc.).
- They don't evaluate while they are observing; they simply take in what they see.
- They keep the context and larger picture in mind at all times.
- They don't clutter the air waves by talking too much.
- They observe with an open mind and don't let past experiences color their thinking.
- They listen to their intuition.
- They are skilled at asking questions which help them understand what they are observing.
- They give people the benefit of the doubt.

When you are observing your people, you need to find some way of keeping track of what you observe. Your observations are the clues about the person and his performance. Clues which when examined together will help you remain objective and see the bigger picture.

The Perceptions of Others

How other people perceive the person you are coaching is important information. It says something about how well she is able to relate to others and what kind of a team player the person is. But don't take everything you hear at face value. Very often people's perceptions of another person are more about themselves than about the other person. Most people's perceptions are fairly subjective. Nevertheless, it is a fact that people feel a certain way so these perceptions must be considered. Sometimes they are right on target. Under any circumstances, perceptions must be dealt with, particularly when they are negative.

It's very important that we not judge people solely on what other people say about them and that we not be too heavily influenced by what any one person says. What we are looking for are themes that we hear from others that can give us some clues about the person. But even here we must be careful. Sometimes a group of people can band together and create a story about a person that is only partially true or altogether untrue. Groups of people can be off base about a person and do that person great harm. The party line can easily become the only line about the person. People can get labeled and never be able to break out of it because the case against them has already been decided.

There are different ways of gathering people's perceptions about a person. Often people will volunteer information. When they do, it's best not to agree or disagree. Simply listen and ask questions which can help you get an idea of where the feedback is really coming from. Is a person, for example, saying something negative about one of your people so that he can look superior? Is the person negative about everyone and everything? Is she setting the other person up to be the scapegoat for something that went wrong for which someone else or the whole group should take responsibility? Or is the person sincere and honest in the feedback and trying to be helpful?

Sometimes you can get information about one of your people by asking your internal customers how well you and your people are servicing them. You can lead the conversation around to finding out who is serving them well and who isn't without looking like you are trying to get the goods on one or more of your people. Ask the customer to give you examples of things your area is doing well and things you need to improve upon. It doesn't have to be an internal customer. It could be an external customer or simply an area of the company with which the person frequently interacts.

There are more formal ways to find out how people are perceived. One of the best ways is to use a multirater system, such as a 360-degree feedback process which we mentioned earlier. (See Further Reading at the back of this book to learn more about 360-degree multirater systems.) It's particularly helpful when everyone participates in the process, including you. That way, no one feels singled out and people are less defensive. If you use such a system it must be positioned properly and it's best to keep the responses of the people doing the rating confidential. If the process isn't managed properly it can do people great harm and it can actually damage strained relationships even further.

We once had a client who misused the 360-degree interview process by interviewing approximately 50 people for each person. They interviewed the person's family, personal friends, former company employees, former bosses—he took it to extremes. He went too far back into the person's past. Sometimes the past is not a good predictor of the future. It is best to stick with the people with whom the person is currently working.

Many people are quite frightened by the idea of hearing what others think of them. A good many people would just rather not know. Most of us are doing our best, so news that doesn't fit our image of ourselves can be disturbing. Self-esteem is what's on the line here. If everyone had a healthy sense of self-esteem none of this would present a problem, but because studies show that the majority of Americans suffer from low self-esteem, this is an area which must be handled very delicately.

Our experience is that one-on-one interviews are superior to written questionnaires when it comes to getting an accurate picture of how others perceive a person. An interviewer can do a better job of finding out how a certain perception was formed and why people feel a certain way. An interviewer can also assess the intensity of emotion behind people's evaluation of the person, which helps one understand the true impact of a person's behavior on others. Also, people can be somewhat nonchalant when filling out a form. They are more likely to give careful thought to their answers when they are sitting across from a live person who is reminding them of how important their honest opinions are they are. It is also harder to lie and twist the truth to a live person than it is to a piece of paper.

The skill of the interviewer is key to getting an accurate picture of people's perceptions. Here's a partial list of what interviewers should do. Most of these apply whether you are doing a formal or informal interview.

- Assure people that what they say will be held in confidence unless they give permission to share the information.
- Explain to the person that you are interviewing her so that you can provide the person in question with information that will help him grow and develop. It is not for the purpose of singling him out or punishing him.
- Be objective in your questioning. Don't ask questions that give the person any clue that you are seeking a certain answer.
- Ask open-ended questions that require more than a yes or no answer.
- Do not react to what people say. Remain the objective fact finder.
- Ask people to give specific examples when they make a general statement about a person.
- Look people directly in the eye when asking questions and observe their body language when they give their response.
- Ask questions that are relevant to the person's job performance.

- Ask the person you are interviewing to watch for positive changes in the other person and acknowledge the change to the person in an affirming way when she sees it.

One of the interviewer's primary jobs is to remain judgment free. If you are doing the interviewing, your focus should be on trying to understand *how* certain perceptions are formed and the dynamics that go on between the person and other people. Be careful that you don't fall into the trap of labeling people one way or another based on the feedback others give you, positive or negative.

People, for example, might perceive another person as being aloof or above it all when in truth the person is just shy. The person may lean toward introversion, which is neither positive or negative, but others perceive him negatively. From the feedback you could come to the conclusion that the person has a superiority complex. Instead, you want to find out *why* people perceive the person in a certain way. What are the behaviors the person is exhibiting? That's the kind of helpful feedback people need—not labeling but an understanding of what they are doing to create perceptions that are working against them in getting the job done.

Here's what an excerpt from a sample interview might look like. The manager is interviewing a colleague in another department who works with the person being assessed.

Manager: Hi, Julie. I'm looking for ways that my department can serve your area better. I'm doing 360-degree interviews for the people in my area so they can grow, develop, and better perform the responsibilities of their job. I know you work closely with Mark. I'd like to ask you a few questions about your working relationship with him. Your feedback will be confidential unless you tell me I can share something with him. The information you provide will help me help Mark reach more of his potential. I'd appreciate hearing any positive comments you have to share as well as constructive criticism.

Julie: Well, I'm glad you asked because I find Mark very hard to work with. Whenever I call him for something, he acts like he is really annoyed with me for asking. And then he gives me a big song and dance about when he can get back to me. I also think he's got a problem with women because he doesn't seem to do that with the men in my department who make requests of him. Maybe he's just a chauvinist. I don't know, but I wish you could assign someone else to work with me.

Manager: Can you give me some examples of times when he was unresponsive to your requests and failed to meet them?

Julie: Well, he always seems to eventually come through for me but it's like pulling teeth to get anything from him. Again, I think he's got a problem working with women.

Manager: So, he meets your requests but it's how he talks to you that bothers you?

Julie: Yes, he's got an attitude.

Manager: Well, tell me exactly what he does that annoys you. Can you give me some examples?

Julie: No, trust me. He's got an attitude.

Manager: Julie, I need you to be specific. I can't help Mark or you if I don't have some concrete examples.

Julie: Well, the other day I asked him if he could run some numbers for me for a marketing presentation I am giving. I told him I needed the numbers that afternoon and he hit the ceiling. He raised his voice to me and said I wasn't the only person making requests of him. He asked if I had ever heard of the word *planning*. He said he needed more advance notice. Well, he got me the numbers but like always it was painful getting them. I was upset the rest of the day.

Manager: Do you think your request was unreasonable? Could you have given him a little advance notice?

Julie: No, because my boss was the one who told me I had to have them that afternoon.

Manager: Did you tell him that?

Julie: No.

Manager: What makes you think he doesn't like women? Has he done anything or made any inappropriate comments that would lead you to believe that?

Julie: No, not really. It's just the way he talks to me. It's the only reason I can think of that would explain why he talks to me in such a way.

Manager: Is there anything else you would like to tell me, Julie?

Julie: No, that's about it.

Manager: Thank you very much. By the way, if you see any changes in Mark, it might be a good idea to let him know.

In this interview you can see that the manager was careful to probe for information so that he could understand what was behind the general statements Julie was making. He did not accept anything at face value and encouraged Julie to back up her comments with specifics. The manager was careful not to give any opinions but through questioning encouraged Julie to think about why Mark had reacted strongly—not that that justifies the comments made by Mark. The manager always kept the interview positive even though Julie had a lot of negative feelings.

Information through Assessment Tools

Sometimes your observations of a person and the feedback you get from others is just not enough. There's a missing piece. You still don't quite understand a person. That's when you may want to consider using an assessment tool.

Actually, even if you think you know a person and can trust the feedback you are getting from others, assessment tools can still be very beneficial. They can be particularly helpful in getting people to embrace the feedback you are giving them. Approximately 90 percent of the executives we coach respond very favorably to the assessment tools once they receive the results. They are amazed at how insightful and objective the tools are in their descriptions of themselves. More and more assessment tools are being used to determine people's strengths instead of just their weaknesses, which has helped change people's perception of assessment tools.

A good assessment tool can provide a useful framework for organizing and discussing behaviors you have observed and the feedback you have received from others. It's a highly objective source of information that people have difficulty arguing with because they themselves provided the input for the test. Because there are no right or wrong answers and no judgments attached to the results, when presented properly, formal assessments can be a less threatening form of feedback.

What Assessment Tools Measure

An assessment tool is an empirically valid and reliable test which can measure any number of things. In the workplace, assessment tools are most frequently used to measure ability, interests, and personality. Those measuring ability can help predict how well one will be able to perform cognitive tasks that are critical to the person's success in a given job. Assessments measuring interests can predict how satisfied one will be in a particular job by assessing his interests in a variety of professions. Personality assessments measure a person's character traits and behaviors in a wide range of situations which can predict how successful one may be in a given job. All three of these types of assessments can be used to assess people for possible hire or promotion as well as for coaching people in their current job. Here's a list of some of the commonly used tests in each of the three categories.

1. *Ability, aptitudes, and skills*
   - Wechsler Adult Intelligence Scale-III
   - The Short Employment tests
   - Wonderlic Personnel Test
2. *Interests*
   - Jackson Vocational Interest Survey
   - Strong Interest Inventory
   - Career Assessment Inventory
3. *Personality*
   - Edward Personal Preference Schedule
   - Minnesota Multiphasis Personality Inventory
   - Myers-Brigg Type Indicator
   - Rorschach Inkblot Technique
   - Sixteen Personality Factor Questionnaire

Some of the tools listed above in each of the three categories must be ordered and administered by a licensed psychologist. Some other tools, such as DISC and I SPEAK, can be ordered and administered by people who may not be licensed psychologists. These tools can be helpful in providing you with a broad framework for understanding people's personality style and behavior. They are low cost, easy to administer, and are especially useful when you give them to an entire team as a way of helping people improve their process skills and teamwork. (See Further Reading at the back of this book for more information on assessment tools.)

When to Use Assessment Tools

When selecting an assessment tool, it is important that you determine with the psychologist up front exactly what you wish to find out. Here are some of the situations in which assessment tools and an effective psychologist can be invaluable.

- A person is having difficulty performing the job and you aren't sure why.
- You are considering the person for another position and aren't sure if she is suited well enough for the job.
- You are having difficulty motivating the person.
- You don't feel you have a good grasp of the person's strengths and weaknesses.
- You are new to your management position, you have some tough goals to reach in a short period of time, and you need to know what kind of team you have to work with.
- You are having difficulty coaching and talking to a person and want to know what approach works best with him.
- You are having difficulty reading the person and want greater insight into her personality and tendencies.

Rules for Using Assessment Tools

There is a lot of gray area when you are dealing with people, but there are guidelines which should *always* by followed when using assessment tools.

- Make sure you know what you want to find out in advance.
- Always explain to the person why he is being asked to complete the assessment—let the person know there are no right or wrong answers. Assure the person that the results will be used to help his development and won't be used against him.

- Keep the results of the assessment strictly confidential between you, the psychologist, and human resources.
- Never make decisions solely on the basis of the assessment.
- Make sure you are working with a skilled, licensed psychologist who fits with the culture of your organization.
- Never use the information to label or pigeonhole people, and when administering assessments to an entire team, encourage them to do the same.

Regardless of how accurate an assessment tool is, it is only as good as the person evaluating the results. It's usually best to have the psychologist give the results to the individual without you present. People are very vulnerable when receiving such feedback and to have two people watching their reactions can be too much pressure. We will talk more about giving feedback in the next chapter.

Putting the Pieces Together

As you can see, before you can give people feedback effectively, you have to gather a lot of information from a lot sources over a sufficient period of time—and you have to keep doing it. As you gather the information you must evaluate it and put it in a framework which will support your efforts to give the person constructive feedback. As you get the information, how do you communicate it? That's the topic of the next chapter.

We began this chapter with the idea that the entire coaching process rests on your ability to get to the truth and to give people feedback that is objective, based in fact, and balanced. Here's a checklist to help you determine if you have effectively gathered information which is relevant and important to their performance and development.

Checklist for Information Gathering

1. Do you regularly drop by the person's work station to say hello and see how the person is doing?
   Yes ☐   No ☐

2. Are you aware of any biases you might have which could affect how you view a person and her performance? Do you work to keep your biases in check?
   Yes ☐   No ☐

3. Have you clearly communicated your expectations to the person? Do you seek information that is relevant to your expectations?
   Yes ☐   No ☐

4. Have you made a conscious effort to get to know the person?
   Yes ☐   No ☐

5. Do you sometimes create opportunities that will allow you to observe the person more closely (e.g., working on a project with him)?
   Yes ☐   No ☐

6. Do you keep your eyes and ears open at all times and watch for small nuances?
   Yes ☐   No ☐

7. As you are observing the person's performance, do you keep the context, culture, and larger picture in mind at all times?
   Yes ☐   No ☐

8. Are you careful to keep track of your observations of the person's performance and the feedback you receive about her from others?
   Yes ☐   No ☐

9. When you are observing the person, do you keep an open mind and refrain from letting past experiences affect your objectivity in the present?
   Yes ☐   No ☐

10. Are you careful not to take everything people say at face value?
    Yes ☐   No ☐

11. Do you refrain from giving your opinion when you are inquiring about others' perceptions of the person?
    Yes ☐   No ☐

12. When you observe a behavior or receive feedback about a person from someone else, do you probe for more information by asking appropriate questions?
Yes ☐   No ☐

13. Do you make use of assessment tools when you feel you don't understand a person or are having difficulty working with him?
Yes ☐   No ☐

14. Are you careful to keep your observations of the person to yourself?
Yes ☐   No ☐

15. Do you go outside your area to seek information about how well a person is performing (if appropriate)?
Yes ☐   No ☐

Scoring: If you answered yes to 13 or more questions, you probably know your people well and you have the information you need to assess them fairly.

If you answered yes to 9 to 12 questions, you are making a good effort to know your people but you may not have a complete enough picture of them and their performance to evaluate them fairly.

If you answered yes to fewer than 9 questions, it's highly unlikely that you have the information you need to assess your people fairly and objectively.

PERSONAL APPLICATION CORNER

One of the common pitfalls of personal relationships is putting people in a box—labeling and stereotyping them in such a way that no matter what they do, they can never get out of the box. Spouses and children are often prime candidates for stereotyping.

We constantly seek information that will justify our view of a person which keeps us from seeing the whole person. No one is all good or all bad. The information is often distorted, exaggerated, and taken out of context. It's no wonder people don't change when we spend so much energy looking for reasons to hold on to our cast-in-stone judgments.

Something to Try: Go back to the Personal Action Corner in Chapter 2. Take the same relationship you worked on and ask yourself these five questions:

1. What kinds of labels have I attached to the person?
2. What are some instances in which I jumped to conclusions about something she did which proved to be incorrect?
3. Is it possible that some of the qualities I don't like about the person are qualities I see in myself?
4. How do I react when others try to defend the person and present a picture of the person that is different from how I see him?
5. How badly do I want to improve the relationship? What would happen if I gave up my labels and started looking for the good in her?

For the next week, concentrate on looking for the good in the person you have selected. Every morning when you arise or at some time during the day, take ten minutes alone by yourself to think about the person. Close your eyes and hold a picture of that person in your mind. Think of the struggles he may be having. See the person behaving towards you and/or others as you would like them to. As you go through the week, look for any good things about the person you find and write them down on a piece of paper. At the end of the week, review your notes. See if you feel differently about the person. The idea is to give the person a chance by seeing him more objectively.

CHAPTER FOUR

STEP 2
Give Feedback

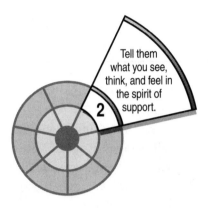

Tell them what you see, think, and feel in the spirit of support.

When you tell people the truth about their performance and where they stand, you relieve them of the pain of ambiguity which builds trust between you.

Some time ago, we were conducting a workshop for a group of managers on the subject of coaching for high performance. We were talking about the fact that people need constructive feedback on an ongoing, consistent basis—what you told them during their performance reviews eight months ago doesn't hold much water because a lot has happened since that time. A man in the class raised his hand and said: "I disagree. People know when they are doing a good job or not. I don't have to constantly tell them. Furthermore," he said, "people know where they stand with me in my personal and professional life. I don't have to tell them."

A young woman on the other side of the class raised her hand and asked the man, "Are you married?" He said, "Yes, I am." She said, "Do you tell your wife you love her?" He said, "Yeah, I told her about 15 years ago and if anything changes I will let her know."

We laugh at the logic of this man, but how often do we assume that people know what we think and feel, at work and in our personal lives? We carry on this inner dialogue within ourselves and forget that others aren't mind readers. Sometimes it is what is *not* said that hurts relationships more than what is said.

We all have a basic need to know where we stand with the people we care about. You may not particularly like your boss but the likelihood is you care very much what she thinks of you and your performance because your livelihood and career are dependent upon it—in the present moment at least. If you are like most people, you need positive feedback to keep the demons of self-doubt at bay.

When people don't receive feedback they feel as if they are lost in space. Many people report to us that they feel invisible because they get absolutely no feedback. Nobody seems to even care or notice that they are there. Others say the only time they hear anything is when they have done something wrong. In either situation, energy and motivation is usually sapped right out of people when they don't get constructive feedback. They are once again back in that pain of ambiguity that we spoke about in Chapter 3, not knowing whether they are setting the world on fire or they are going to be out on the street because nobody gives them a clue about how well they are performing.

If you are one who still isn't quite sure if all this coaching and feedback is worth the time and effort, just remember these three simple facts:

1. People cannot change unless you tell them what they need to change.
2. People want to succeed. What they say and do makes very good sense to them even if it looks off base and absurd to you.
3. You cannot grow a business unless you grow the people.

Frequency of Feedback

In Chapter 3 we covered Step 1 in the process, seek the truth. We talked about the importance of constantly observing your people and gathering objective information about their behavior and performance. Step 2, giving feedback, is the activity which drives The 7 Steps to Trust-Based Management process which means you should constantly be giving feedback at every step along the way.

Actually, none of the seven steps should be performed in isolation. The entire process should constantly be in motion for each of your people. (Your boss should be doing the same for you.) One moment you might be observing some aspect of a person's behavior, the next day you might be celebrating one of his accomplishments, and the next you might be working with the person's resistance to seeing some aspect of his behavior. The steps don't always happen in the sequence we have presented in the model.

The key is to give *constant* feedback and give it close to the time of the event. The executives we coach often lament that not only is the feedback they receive negative, lacking in objectivity, and void of any specifics, it is rarely given on a timely basis. They report that the feedback is meaningless when they can't recall the details of a situation in question because it was such a long time ago. One executive we coached said he once got feedback about something he had done two years after the fact. When people receive surprises of this nature it destroys trust. They feel they are being blindsided. Most people hate nothing more than to be told for the first time during their annual performance review about something they have done. Feedback should be given as close to the time of the event as humanly possible.

A feedback session can take any number of forms from the annual performance review to an on-the-job observation of the person followed by immediate feedback and coaching. There is no rule that says you should meet with your people a specific number of times but it should not be restricted to once or twice a year.

It is always amazing to us in our coaching practice how few managers understand the fact that they are *always* giving feedback of some kind. Two executives in particular were totally oblivious to the fact that people are constantly observing their every move. It was shocking news to them.

How you walk, how you greet people, how you dress, how you drink your coffee—everything you do and say speaks to how people perceive you. In the workplace many people have a tendency to overpersonalize what the boss says and does, so it's safe to assume that just about everything you do is interpreted as feedback of sorts, whether you intend it as such or not. In this book, of course, when we talk about giving people feedback, we are talking about time that is set aside for the express purpose of reflecting back to people what you see, think, and feel about their performance.

Here are five questions to help you determine if you are giving your people enough feedback:

1. Have I withheld any important information from the person which is causing me to interact with the person in a negative fashion?
2. Does each person appear to be comfortable and at ease with me or is there an apparent strain in the relationship? Does it feel the person is withholding something from me?

3. Do I periodically take time to sit down with each person and talk only about her performance and development or are all of our conversations directly related to the task at hand?
4. When I give my performance reviews at the end of the year are people surprised by what they hear and see on the form? Are they hearing it for the first time?
5. Do I have a track record of developing and promoting people? Are my people going on to bigger and better things?

If you answered no to any of the above questions, you are probably not giving or getting enough feedback from your people.

If you are still not sure whether you are giving people enough feedback, ask them. They will be happy to tell you. Request that they be specific. What are some examples of times when you did or didn't give feedback to them and how were they affected by it?

Preparing for a Feedback Session

The effectiveness of any formal feedback session is usually directly related to the amount of preparation you put into it. A feedback session is more than presenting information to people. It's creating an environment, positioning what you wish to communicate, responding in the moment, and dealing with resistance. It requires a lot of forethought and skill if you are to achieve the desired result.

When you are preparing, the first thing you will want to do is ask yourself some questions: What is the result I wish to achieve? What are the objectives I wish to accomplish? What is it I would like the person to understand, feel, and do as a result of our session?

Being clear about your objectives is paramount. Sometimes we may think we have one objective in mind when in fact we have another lurking in the shadows. In our rational mind we know that all feedback sessions should be about helping the person perform better but sometimes our own emotions take over and the session turns into something else. If we don't like a person (and that happens because we are only human) and/or we are particularly angry and upset about something he has done, our real objective may be to punish the person, to put fear into him, or to quickly whip the person into shape. We've said it before and we will say it many times more: You have to be able to get yourself out of the way. If you let your emotions and personal biases rule, you will fail to accomplish your higher objective of encouraging the person to perform better and grow.

▼ OUR EXPERIENCE

The Danger of Personal Bias

We have coached thousands of executives over the years, the vast majority of whom report that they receive little or no feedback. Many of those who do receive feedback report that the feedback is filled with innuendo and provides little instruction of how to rectify their problems. The 360-degree feedback process is one example of how many companies do only half the job. They tell people what the problems are but they don't follow up with any instruction or support.

We worked with one executive who reportedly had a problem working with women. A supervisor who worked with him said he was condescending to women and did not respect their strengths and talents. The supervisor said she had observed such behavior in his interaction with his boss and subordinates and she said she had received feedback to the same effect from other women in the company.

In our 360-degree interview process we are careful not to seek out information that confirms a judgment that has already been made about a person. Our work is something like detective work. Take nothing at face value and keep searching for clues until you get to the bottom of things—until you find the truth. We, too, have to keep a clear screen. Surprisingly, when we interviewed the eight people who worked closely with this particular person, not one of them had anything but complimentary things to say about his treatment of women in the workplace. To make sure we were getting the true picture, we even interviewed his spouse and two daughters who reported that he had always demonstrated respect for women.

From this experience we were reminded of the importance of keeping our objective in mind—our objective of helping the person. It is easy to be influenced by other people who may have other objectives in mind, objectives which may be rooted in their own personal bias. Correct motives or objectives are the foundation of every successful feedback session.

—Bill

Some of your feedback objectives may change, but with every feed-back session there are three objectives which should always be a part of your agenda:

1. To provide the person with objective information about her per-formance and/or behavior which will empower the person to grow and reach more of her potential
2. To help the person understand the significance and impact of his behavior and performance on other people and the company
3. To build self-esteem and confidence as much as possible

If you don't make a conscious effort to stay focused on your higher objectives, you can easily get off track. If a person doesn't like what you are saying and begins to attack you, for example, you can assume a de-fensive posture if you aren't careful and go on the attack yourself which will accomplish nothing. In Chapter 6 we will go into great detail about how to break through the resistance, but for now, just remember how important it is to stay on your own thread and never lose sight of what you are trying to achieve. Stay consistent when people try to pull you off balance. That's why it's important to prepare yourself for how you will handle the various possible responses.

When you prepare, you will want to have a loose outline of how you plan to conduct the session. We say loose because every feedback ses-sion should be a dialogue. You can't plan a dialogue. It requires respond-ing in the moment. The outline can serve as a road map for keeping you on track but it should be flexible enough to allow for a few detours along the way. Once you are clear on what your objectives for the ses-sion are, here are some questions to help you in your planning.

- How will I begin the session? What can I do and say to help the person feel relaxed and open?
- What should the desired outcome look like?
- What kinds of facts, observations, and feedback will I use to ac-complish the objectives I have set? What examples do I have to draw from?
- How can I engage the person so I can understand what she is really thinking and feeling? How can I help to reduce the person's defensiveness so she can hear what I am saying?

- What kinds of reactions do I anticipate and how will I respond to them?
- How will I know if the person is receiving my feedback?
- When I am concluding the session, how can I affirm the person and make very clear what I want him to do after he leaves?

Setting the Stage

When you get a telephone call from your boss and she says, "I would like to see you in my office tomorrow at 2 PM," what is the first thought that goes through your mind? For many people, the response in their head is, "What did I do wrong?" Most people don't look at feedback sessions as something positive, something that can help them. Perhaps it's because too many of us haven't worked under bosses who know how to make them a positive experience. That's why you must work particularly hard at creating a safe, comfortable environment—physically and psychologically.

When you schedule the session, let them know that you would like to give them some feedback about their performance and that you are open to hearing any feedback they may have to give you. This way you are helping to equalize the power and are sending the message that this is a two-way street. It is not a session for hand slapping and telling them what they have done wrong.

When you schedule the session, make sure it is at a time when you are at your best. If you are not a morning person, don't do it at 8 AM. And don't do it when you are rushed. Maybe you are always rushed; but if you are constantly getting up and down during the session and answering the telephone you will convey a very loud message—the person you are meeting with is not very important. There is no greater way to convey respect to a person than by giving him your total, complete, undivided attention. If you want him to take what you say seriously, you must treat the session seriously. There are very few things that should interrupt your feedback session.

The place you choose to have the session should be comfortable and most important, nonthreatening. Depending upon the relationship, you may want to conduct it in a conference room that is neutral territory. If you have a good relationship with the person already and you have it in your office, make sure you don't sit behind your desk. Your desk is a power symbol and a barrier. Instead, pull up two chairs or sit at a table.

When you start the meeting, take a few minutes to put the person at ease. Sometimes it's a good idea to begin talking about something totally unrelated to work. If she plays a sport like tennis or golf, ask her how her game is these days. The key is to establish some kind of rapport before you begin. A certain amount of small talk at the beginning will also give you time to do some quick assessment in your mind as to how the person may be feeling about the session. Is he cool and distant? Is she particularly nervous? Remember, you want to follow your plan but you also have to play it by ear and respond in the moment.

Before you get into the giving of feedback, you want to remind him of the purpose of the meeting. You might say something like: "The reason I wanted to meet with you is to give you some specific feedback on your performance and behavior. I'm, of course, interested in how you are performing because my success depends on it, but I am also concerned and interested in you as a person. I want you to have a positive work experience here. Your growth and development is as important to me as I know it is to you.

"We all need feedback. I receive it regularly from my boss and others and if I don't get it I ask for it, because I need that information in order to know what to do differently—so that I am always clear on what is expected of me. We all have blind spots that we need help with, myself included.

"During our session today, I would also like some feedback from you. Our session today should be two-way. I'm particularly interested in hearing your thoughts on how you think I can support you better."

Never begin a session with a criticism right off the bat. That is the quickest way to put people on the defensive. The key is to relax them, position the session as something positive, and set it up from the beginning as a two-way conversation rather than a monologue from you.

Tell Them What You See, Think, and Feel

Once you have set the stage for the session, you will begin to give your feedback. It's usually a good idea to begin by affirming the person in some way, by giving her some positive feedback. The purpose of this is not to manipulate her so that you can get the medicine down. The purpose of the positive feedback up front is to provide some balance and perspective. Studies show that two out of three Americans suffer from low self-esteem. People who don't have a healthy sense of self-esteem frequently respond internally to negative feedback by indicting themselves beyond what the true feedback implies. If you give them positive and negative feedback, most people will focus on the negative.

For example, let's say a boss says to an employee "I think we need to spend some time focusing on your communication skills and here are the reasons why." If he is lacking in self-esteem, he will sometimes use this information against himself and distort what you have said. You have not said you are displeased with his performance. You have not said he is a loser. You have not said he is going to lose his job. But for many people, that is what they hear when they receive a criticism because they are so accustomed to seeing themselves in a negative light. They don't see their own strengths and weaknesses in a balanced light so anything negative is exaggerated in their minds, and then, of course, they outwardly deny it. That's what so much of the resistance is about. So to reduce the resistance, start with something positive but make it sincere. The key is to give the person a balanced perspective.

Most people need to be convinced that they can change. If the feedback is only negative, people will often give up in despair because nothing they do seems to be right. They feel they have no positive base to build upon.

We were asked to coach an executive once who had received nothing but negative feedback over time. Interestingly, his behavior did not change one bit and he was eventually terminated. By building such a strong case against him and constantly presenting that case to him, his superiors actually reinforced the behaviors they were trying to correct. Another executive we coached actually enjoyed giving people negative feedback which was the only kind he ever gave. He prided himself in being brutally honest which only served to destroy all trust between himself and his people. As a result, there was no foundation for the behavior changes he was seeking.

When you tell someone what you see, make sure you focus on the behavior and the performance, not the person. As you give her the feedback, involve her in dialogue. Ask her what she thinks of the feedback you are giving her. Your feedback should also be given in the context of the objectives, standards, and expectations that have been set for the person and should be referred to regularly. They are essential because they are the criteria against which you should be evaluating the person. If you have unfair or unclear expectations, you cannot give effective feedback. You will only confuse and demotivate the person.

Nothing annoys people more than when a manager makes broad general statements about them and their performance and doesn't back it up with examples. Here's where you must have done your homework. You must have the facts in front of you. Those facts may consist of direct observations you have made, examples of work, and measures of productivity (e.g., actual amount of work completed in a given period). The facts may also consist of feedback you have received from others. When you give them the feedback from others, remember to tell them that the reported perceptions of others may not be fact but it is a fact that people feel a certain way. And, of course, if you have given them any of the assessments we mentioned in Chapter 3, you can cite examples from the test results.

People cannot easily argue facts. The more concrete examples you give them, the greater the chance they will understand the point you are trying to make. You are *not* trying to build a case against them by gathering your facts. They will shut down if they feel that is your agenda. You are trying to gather information which can penetrate their mindset and help them see themselves and their performance in a more realistic light. Most important, make sure your words are judgment- and blame-free. The minute you criticize and/or blame you set up an automatic resistance.

When you give feedback, you not only want to tell them what you see but also how you feel about it. Feelings are an important component in the whole coaching process—yours and theirs. If you are not clear about how you feel when it is something you feel strongly about—both positive and negative—the person will leave feeling unsure about himself and the relationship. For example, if you are angry as a hornet about something he has done, you don't want to lash out at him and express your anger inappropriately. But if you don't acknowledge how you feel, the person will try to read into the situation and will once again be in the pain of ambiguity. Feelings are real and must be dealt with.

You can express how you feel without judging the person and without humiliating her. You can simply state, "Mary, I need to tell you that when you don't have regular staff meetings with your people to keep them informed, after I have asked you repeatedly to do so, I am disappointed." Make sure you don't tell her that she disappoints you. Own your own feelings. Simply state them as a fact. You don't want to say something like: "Mary you make me furious when you don't have regular staff meetings. Are you deaf? I have talked to you repeatedly about this issue. You really disappoint me."

When you are angry or upset it's very important that you check in with yourself to make sure you are directing your feelings toward the real source. Misdirected anger can be very damaging. We coached a woman once who was always angry with members of her team. She would berate them unmercifully. Through coaching we found that she was simply an angry person. In truth, she was not particularly angry at the individuals on her team; she was angry about life and it was spilling over onto her team. Once she understood herself better, she was able to leave her feelings about her life at the doorstep. She consequently became a far more effective leader and was able to win back the respect of her team.

When you are giving people feedback, your job is to be a good mirror. A mirror doesn't judge. It doesn't say, "You are fat" or "You are ugly." It simply reflects back what is presented. This is where your objectivity is critical. If you have been clear in your expectations and you've been clear on what the consequences and rewards are for different behaviors and they are fair, you don't have to be the policeman. You simply reflect back what you see, refer back to the expectations, and follow through on the appropriate reward or consequence. It's not always quite this simple, but as a general rule, it's the best way to get results while preserving the relationship. This way the responsibility is on them.

In the sample dialogue below, the manager is telling the employee, Gary, what she sees, thinks, and feels. The manager has set the stage for the meeting and is now into the heart of the coaching session.

Manager: Gary, I know you are interested in being promoted to a supervisory position so I'd like to talk about what needs to happen if you are going to achieve that goal. As I have mentioned before, you have excellent skills and a wealth of technical knowledge. People respect you for what you know. At the same time, I have observed some behaviors and have received feedback from others which leads me to believe that we need to work on your interpersonal skills.

Gary: Here we go. I can only imagine where that has come from— from those lazy people I work with who have nothing better to do than talk about other people. In terms of work output I run circles around them.

Manager: We aren't talking about them. We are talking about you. It's not going to do us any good to focus on other people. The only people we have control over are ourselves. Why don't you hear me out and then you can respond, okay?

Gary: Okay.

Manager: I have seen you on numerous occasions be very short with people when they request something of you or when someone says something you don't agree with. In the staff meeting yesterday, for example, we were discussing the new product introduction and Sam, who is usually very quiet, made a contribution and you said, "That is the most ridiculous idea I have ever heard." Sam closed up and didn't say another word the rest of the meeting. That's just one example. I have received comments from the finance department that when ever they ask you for information you give them a hard time. (Depending on Gary's response, the manager would give more examples.)

Gary: First of all, Sam's idea was a stupid idea and those bean counters in the accounting department are always bugging me for information. Often, it's information they already have. It just seems that there is so much incompetency around here. The people who get ahead are those who play the political game. If you work hard and press to get results for the company, you get reprimanded.

Manager: The world is not a perfect place. People are not perfect. If you are going to achieve your goal of becoming a supervisor you must pay as much attention to how you deal with people as you do to getting the job done. People respect you for what you know and for your technical skills, Gary, but they don't respect you when you put them down and don't cooperate with them.

Gary: So what do I do when the accounting department keeps bugging me for information that I've already given them and they give me these unreasonable deadlines? You know I am under so much pressure in this department because the rest of the folks are not pulling their share.

Manager: In regard to the accounting department, if they have asked you for the same information before, you could say nicely, "I gave you that information last week. Do you remember?"

Gary: I tried that. It doesn't work.

Manager: Okay. In the future when that happens, tell me about it and I will talk to their boss about it. But, there is a bigger issue here. I must tell you what I am seeing and hearing. You don't appear to be open to looking at ways you can improve. You keep focusing on and blaming other people.

Gary: Well, I'm just tired of trying. I've worked for this company for eight years and you keep telling me what a good job I am doing and how valuable I am to the company. So if that is true, why haven't I been promoted?

Manager: Gary, you do have a lot to offer and you make a lot of wonderful contributions, but you undermine your own success by the way you treat people. The way you are treating me right now is a perfect example. You are closed to hearing anything I have to say or to looking at yourself. Do you want to be a team player? Do you want to have good relationships with your colleagues?

Gary: Yes, but it takes two to tango.

Manager: You know, I've always found that if one person tells me something about myself, it may or may not be true. It could be their problem. But if it is coming from more than one place, there is usually at least a grain of truth in it—something I need to look at if I am going to grow. Look, I know this is not easy. None of us, myself included, wants to look at our weaknesses. None of us is perfect. I think you have a lot of potential but it's being thwarted by these behavior patterns that keep repeating themselves. Are you willing to try some new behaviors to see what kind of results you might get from others? Just try?

Gary: Okay.

Manager: One of the things that will help with your peers in the department is to find some way to affirm them individually. It doesn't have to be anything too overt. As I have said, people respect you for your knowledge and experience. If you were to ask their opinions or ask them for some help in a nice way from time to time, I think it would go a long way in helping them see you as a part of the team. It will help each of them feel that you value them as a person. Periodically, when you need a break from work, stop by their desks or offices and sit down and chat for a few minutes about anything but work. Let people see another side of you. Let them get to know you a little better.

Gary: But I am not here to win a popularity contest. I am here to work—to get the job done. That seems like a total waste of time.

Manager: Relationships are the basis of everything. You need those people to accomplish your own objectives and the objectives of the team. If you have no rapport with them, they will have no interest in supporting you in your efforts. Plus, it makes work so much more enjoyable when you have good working relationships. Will you at least be open to trying it?

Gary: Okay.

Manager: When it comes to requests from other departments, if you find yourself getting angry or stressed by their requests, don't respond immediately. Probe to find out what they need and ask them if you can get back to them within a certain period of time. This will buy you some time so you can collect yourself, look at your workload, and respond more rationally. If it is an unreasonable request or you don't see how you can meet your own deadline and the deadline for the request, come see me and we will work it out together. Does that seem reasonable?

Gary: Yes.

Manager: What else can I do to help you?

Gary: Nothing.

Manager: I want you to understand how important this is. All of us in this company are expected to treat one another with respect. It is especially important for you if you want to become a supervisor. I want you to try these behaviors for the next three weeks at which time we will reconvene to see how you are doing. In fact, let's set a date right now.

In the above example, the manager kept affirming the person while she was confronting him with information about his behavior. The likelihood is that the person wants very much to be a part of the team but doesn't know how. From his previous behavior, one would guess that he has had this problem for a long time. While he is quite confident in his skills and abilities, when it comes to people he is probably insecure which is what all the posturing and criticism is about. Instead of feeding his insecurity, the manager tells him she believes in him and tries to help him. She resists the temptation to return negative energy with more negative energy. Not an easy thing to do but essential. At the same time, she tells him the truth and is clear about what she expects.

Keeping Them Engaged

Have you ever been the recipient of feedback from a boss who did all of the talking? He steamrolled through the session while you sat there like a silent bump on a log? How did you feel about it? What did it do for your self-esteem and how open were you to hearing what he had to say?

One of the messages we send when we do all the talking and neglect to engage the person is that the way we see it is the way it is and there is no room for changing our minds. When we don't involve them in the assessment of the problem or the development of solutions and courses of action, we communicate that their opinions don't count. Case closed. This is the way it is and this is what I want you to do about it. If your feedback sessions approach anything close to this, they will be disasters.

You should ask each person what she thinks of her performance. The more open and flexible you remain, the more likely the person will listen to what you have to say because she believes she has a chance to be heard. Managers often get ahead of themselves when they are giving their people feedback. They tell the person, for example, how they want him to change before the person has even agreed that he has a problem or that his performance needs improvement.

The first goal of any feedback session should be to create understanding. You want them to understand something about themselves or their performance. Sometimes managers are the ones who need a better understanding of the person and situation. Regardless of how well you think you have gathered your facts and information and how carefully you have studied them, you can still be wrong. There may be some information you don't know that could affect how you see the person and the situation at hand. If you think of it as an exploration—together asking questions which can help you come to some agreement about her behavior and performance—you are much more likely to get her buy-in and ultimately the behavior change you are seeking. The more supportive you are of them the less defensive they will be.

You can get them in dialogue with you by asking questions such as: What's your view of what I just said? Is there something about the situation that I don't know that you would like to share with me? Do you agree with what I just said? Why do you think I've gotten the feedback I have from other people? Do you have any idea how these perceptions might have been formed? How are you feeling right now? What do you think you can do to make things better? How can I help you?

The key is to keep them in dialogue with you throughout the session. When you are presenting your initial feedback about a particular point, you may want to ask them to remain quiet until you have finished and then you will listen to them. This way each of you can be heard without constantly interrupting one another. Sometimes you will have to work very hard at drawing people out. One of the most common defenses is to shut down. We will talk more in Chapter 6 about how to read what is going on with people and how to draw them out.

Be Direct and to the Point

We coached the president of a corporation once who on our first meeting spent 1½ hours convincing us that he gives direct, honest feedback to his direct reports. He proceeded to tell us in specific detail what he had told them. When we spoke with his people during the 360-degree interviews, every one of them said they had *not* heard anything close to what the boss told us he said to them. Oh, how we delude ourselves! This happens time and again. The boss says he gave honest, direct feedback and the people say, "No he didn't."

Those of us who have a difficult time with confrontation (which seems to be the majority of people) can easily miss the boat when we are giving feedback. Sometimes managers either water down the feedback or dance around the problem to the point that the person never gets it. When this happens our intentions are usually good but don't help anyone very much. And then we wonder why the person doesn't change. Sometimes managers will be direct and then quickly take back what they have said when they see the person getting upset.

Our intent should never be to hurt people. In fact, if you are going to effectively coach people you need a lot of compassion. The thing many people forget is that you can tell people the truth and still be compassionate. It doesn't mean people aren't going to feel bad at times. It doesn't mean you aren't going to be uncomfortable at times. If people are going to grow, they must hear the truth and sometimes the truth hurts. You are not responsible for their feelings. Most of the time we need to let people sit with their feelings—let them sink in. That goes for positive feedback as well as negative. Those feelings can often serve as the motivation to change.

Many of us feel that when we get negative feedback we are going to be rejected as a person because that's what we have come to believe from our past experience. For a lot of people it is a whole new experience to be given negative feedback in a way that doesn't attack who they are as a person, and then on the heals of that negative feedback, to be accepted and affirmed. That is liberating and healing for people because it says to them that we are all human—that it's okay to be imperfect.

▼ **OUR EXPERIENCE**

Practicing What We Preach

In our coaching business we work very hard at giving each other constructive feedback which sometimes isn't an easy thing to do. We know that a good coach never falls into the trap of thinking he has it all together. We too are human and sometimes have blind spots that we need to have mirrored to us. And when that happens it is not always a pretty picture. It's not easy looking at our own weaknesses.

Diane and I had such an experience right in the middle of the time we were working on this book together. We were immersed in thinking and writing about coaching concepts when, all of a sudden, we were faced with the task of applying them to each other.

I asked Diane if she would go on a sales call to one of our clients who had a prospective coaching job. She was to meet with the human resource representative first and then with the candidate. The client is known for being somewhat demanding and difficult. Anyway, we were talking on the telephone the day after the sales call about some edits on the manuscript when the subject of the sales call came up. I delivered some very pointed, negative feedback to her which the client had given to me. While the client was off base in some of her feedback about Diane, Diane knew there was some truth in what had been said and that she needed to hear it.

When I gave Diane the feedback, much to my surprise, I could hear she was very upset. "What?" I said. "You are better than that!"

Immediately, I asked Diane, "Okay, now you give me feedback. What did I do wrong? How could I have given it to you in such a way that you wouldn't be so upset by it?" Her response that day and even the next day when we both had time to think about what had happened was, "Nothing."

As Diane explained, "I needed to hear what you told me—the unvarnished, honest feedback, even though it was painful. It's the pain and the owning of what was said that will make me change. If you had softened it and beaten around the bush, I would have sensed that you were withholding something from me which would have worried me and left me confused and I may have missed the point."

I do think I should have waited to deliver the feedback face-to-face. I was also not clear about the fact that the feedback had not come from the prospective coachee and the human resource professional. It was only from the human resource professional. When Diane and I spoke later, I also learned of some of the details about the meeting which helped me understand better why Diane had reacted so strongly. That experience actually helped to strengthen our working relationship. I'm sure my turn is coming.

—Bill

Don't Sweat the Small Stuff

Make sure the feedback you provide is not only relevant but important. Nitpicking over unimportant matters is a sure way to drive your people away. You should be able to distinguish between what is irritating to you and what is important to the accomplishment of the job. They are not always the same. Perfectionism is costly and nonproductive. Sure you want people to achieve excellence, but true excellence is compromised when we focus on unimportant matters. Learn to let some things slide. People don't want to feel that they are under a microscope.

And when you ask for behavior changes, don't ask for too many changes at once or too big of a change (unless it is absolutely imperative and appropriate). People change in small increments—not giant steps. If you make the expected behavior change too big you will set them up for failure and demotivate them in their efforts to change. Motivation is a key factor in the change process so you want to keep them in a positive frame of mind as much as possible.

Let's say, for example, that a person has a tendency to talk too much and not listen enough. Instead of saying, " I want you to stop talking so much and be a better listener" you might say instead, "I want you to pay more attention to the body language and cues others may be giving when you are talking and not listening. For the next three days, every time you have a conversation of any significance with someone, I want you to record the gist of the conversation, how much you talked (percentage of time), and what the quality of the interaction felt like." In other words, give the person something to do toward the resolution of the problem, but don't expect him or her to change ingrained patterns of behavior overnight.

When to Wrap It Up

One of the things you want to be careful not to do is to beat a dead horse. In other words, once you have made your point, back off. You don't necessarily need a verbal: "Oh, yes. I was wrong. I see the error of my ways and will change." Usually you will know when a person has gotten the picture.

Also, don't engage in debates with people that go on and on. They are counterproductive. For example, let's say you have been giving feedback to a person about her need to be a better team player. You cite examples of times you have seen her work against the interests of the team and you tell her about feedback you have received from others in relation to this issue, but she consistently denies and/or rationalizes what you are saying. You can see that she is getting more and more upset as she tries to put the focus and blame onto other people. She is so upset that you know she isn't hearing anything you are saying. You are trying very hard to get through to her and now you are getting frustrated and upset because she refuses to listen.

If you have done everything you can to achieve understanding but have been unsuccessful, it may be best to conclude the session and ask the person to think about what has been said and set a date for another meeting. Sometimes people just can't absorb what you are saying when they first hear it. Some people will never be able to accept constructive criticism.

When you conclude the session, make sure you affirm them in some way: recap what you have covered in the meeting, clearly state your expectations in terms of the behavior change(s) you wish to see, and decide how and when you will follow up with one another. Your conclusion might go something like this: "Just to recap, as I mentioned I am very pleased with your performance. You are a real asset to our team. I appreciate your hard work. I do want you to focus on delegating more to your people. As we agreed, during the next two weeks you are going to keep track of the tasks you are doing and you are going to see how many of those you can effectively delegate to others. When you delegate, you are going to make sure you cover the points we discussed. We will meet again two weeks from today at the same time and we will discuss your progress. Is that your understanding? If you have any questions in the meantime, please feel free to check with me."

Anatomy of a Feedback Session

The sequence of a formal feedback session should go something as follows:

1. Put the person at ease.
2. Explain the objectives and purpose of the session and ask him if he understands.
3. Give her some sincere positive feedback as a way of creating balance if you have constructive criticism to deliver.
4. Review the objectives, standards, expectations, etc., of the job if appropriate (depending on what kind of feedback session you are having).
5. Give an objective account of your observations and credible feedback you may have gotten from others.
6. Ask him how he feels about your feedback. Let him respond. Be prepared for him to disagree. Listen openly to what he has to say.
7. Engage her in continued give-and-take dialogue until you come to some agreement about the problem or situation.
8. Brainstorm possible solutions/courses of action and ask him how you can help him.
9. Ask her if she has any feedback for you. Is there anything she would like to share with you that could help you be a better manager?
10. Recap the session, clearly defining your expectations and what the specific behavior change(s) should look like.
11. Affirm him and agree upon how and when you will follow up with one another. Set a specific date and time.

One of the toughest parts of giving effective feedback is dealing with people's resistance—reducing the fear so that in their minds it is okay to admit to an error or shortcoming. One of the most common failures of managers in giving feedback comes from their inability to work with the resistance in a constructive way which is why we will devote Chapter 6 to this topic.

Feedback Self-Evaluation Checklist

As you can see, there is a lot to think about and plan for when you are giving people feedback. If you follow the sequence and guidelines we have provided, after a while it will become second nature. This doesn't mean you don't have to plan, but the whole process will be much less arduous and time consuming and you'll achieve better results because you are more skilled at it. Here is a checklist you can use as a reminder of the things you will want to do when you are giving feedback. It's also a good idea to review this checklist after every feedback session as a way of evaluating how well you did.

1. Did I spend enough time planning for the session?
   Yes ☐   No ☐

2. When I scheduled the meeting did I explain the purpose of the meeting to the person in positive terms?
   Yes ☐   No ☐

3. Did I schedule the meeting at a time when I wasn't rushed and pressed for time? Did I give the person my undivided attention?
   Yes ☐   No ☐

4. Did I hold the meeting at a time and place that was nonthreatening to the person?
   Yes ☐   No ☐

5. Did I put the person at ease at the beginning of the meeting and set an informal tone?
   Yes ☐   No ☐

6. Did I begin the meeting by explaining the purpose of the session in positive terms?
Yes ☐   No ☐

7. Did I affirm the person in some way before I began giving constructive feedback?
Yes ☐   No ☐

8. Did I direct my comments to the behavior and not the person?
Yes ☐   No ☐

9. Was I direct and specific about the behavior and did I give examples?
Yes ☐   No ☐

10. Did I express my thoughts and feelings calmly and respectfully?
Yes ☐   No ☐

11. Did I stay objective and speak from the facts?
Yes ☐   No ☐

12. Was I careful not to threaten the person in any way?
Yes ☐   No ☐

13. Did I engage the person in dialogue and was I open to changing my mind? Did we work on defining and solving the problem together?
Yes ☐   No ☐

14. Did I convey compassion while being honest and direct?
Yes ☐   No ☐

15. Was I careful not to ask for too large a behavior change or too many changes?
Yes ☐   No ☐

16. Did I present a balanced picture of the person's performance?
Yes ☐   No ☐

17. Did I make sure my body language and facial expressions were consistent with my words?
    Yes ☐   No ☐

18. Did I watch for the feeling content of what the person was saying and respond accordingly?
    Yes ☐   No ☐

19. Did I affirm the person whenever I could, especially at the end?
    Yes ☐   No ☐

20. Was I clear about what the behavior change should look like?
    Yes ☐   No ☐

21. If I delivered negative feedback, did I explain the consequences of not changing?
    Yes ☐   No ☐

22. Did I keep the conversation focused? If the person got sidetracked did I bring her back?
    Yes ☐   No ☐

23. Did I ask for the person's feedback on myself?
    Yes ☐   No ☐

24. Did I ask how I could be of assistance to the person?

25. When I concluded the meeting did I clearly state my expectations, recap the course of action to be taken, and set a time for follow up?
    Yes ☐   No ☐

Evaluation: This checklist is to be used primarily as a guide and reminder before you conduct a feedback session and as a basis for evaluating how well you conducted the session when it is over. It is difficult to score this checklist because you could do everything on the list but one thing that could be the very thing that causes the session to be unsuccessful.

PERSONAL ACTION CORNER

Too often in our personal relationships our feedback takes the form of criticism. Think about it. Have you ever accomplished anything in a relationship by criticizing the other person? Have you ever, for example, registered a criticism to your spouse or significant other about something he was doing that you wanted him to change? Did you ever have him come back to you and say, "Oh, thank you, honey. I now know how to be a better person."? Not likely. More often than not, the other person digs his heels in, gets defensive, and levels a criticism right back. It becomes the blame game—who is right and who is wrong.

Most of us don't know how to give honest, constructive feedback in our homes because we never saw it modelled in the families we came from. Did you grow up in a home where everyone in the family was given equal right and opportunity to have an opinion, disagree, and even have some feelings? Could you hash things through to resolution without someone going for the jugular? If you did, you are one of the lucky ones.

Most people in our seminars report that they grew up in homes where only one person was allowed to get angry and when that person got angry everyone else ran for cover and waited for the storm to blow over. The person who got angry was the one who decided when it was over. Everyone woke up the next morning and pretended that nobody said the horrible things that they said, nobody threw the plate of spaghetti across the room. Even though people may have been acting like things were back to normal, they weren't. People carry that unresolved stuff around with them—sometimes for a lifetime. All too often the hurt comes out sideways—sometimes on people who weren't even there.

If you want healthy relationships with the people close to you, you have to keep the air clean. You have to do what we call "love's tough work." You have to address issues as they arise in a way that creates understanding instead of more conflict. Sometimes delivering constructive feedback is painful, but it's not nearly as painful as realizing that a relationship is beyond repair because too many issues have gone unresolved and caused too much hurt over time. The more issues that are allowed to grow, the harder it is to get the relationship back on track.

Something to Try: Once again, think of the relationship you chose to work on in Chapters 2 and 3. Ask yourself these questions:

- What is it I need to tell the person so that we can begin working on the problem(s) in the relationship? What specifics and examples can I give?
- What part of the problem can I take ownership of and admit to the person?
- Why am I so afraid to speak the truth to the person? What do I think will happen if I do? What will happen if I don't?
- Do I sometimes in the moment just want to vent instead of resolve the problem?
- If I have given feedback in the past and it only made matters worse, what can I do to change the way I give feedback so that the other person can understand how I feel without getting defensive?

Set aside a time when you and the person can talk about your relationship and deliver honest, nonjudgmental feedback to each other. Before you begin you might share with the person what you have learned about giving feedback as a way of setting some ground rules. Tell the person you sincerely want to have a better relationship—that you care about her and want to have a better understanding between the two of you. Most of the guidelines we have discussed in this chapter apply to your personal relationships as well. Good luck!

CHAPTER FIVE

STEP 3
Create a Vision and Plan

When you help people
see what they can be and
provide them with a map
for getting there, they
trust you because you have
their interests at heart.

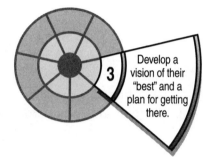

Develop a vision of their "best" and a plan for getting there.

The developmental plan is the road map which is going to take the person from where he is to where he needs to be. If you stopped at Step 2, gave him feedback but didn't give him a developmental plan, it would be like a physician giving a diagnosis without a remedy or treatment plan. In either case, nothing is likely to change. We cannot expect people to change their behavior or improve their competencies without our help.

The developmental plan provides a structured approach to personal change. How many times have you received a performance review that gave you plenty of feedback about your strengths and weaknesses, but the section that was to detail the developmental action steps was sketchy at best? Maybe a few courses were listed but nothing that really focused on changing the behaviors or improving the skills which were identified as needing improvement in the feedback section.

The developmental action plan should also serve as a tool for holding the person accountable. How can you measure her improvement if you don't have a written plan which spells out what she is supposed to do? A good developmental plan should allow you and the person to easily monitor her progress.

The Antidote for Fear

The amount of fear a person has regarding the coaching process depends on the nature of the coaching. There are basically three types of situations:

1. The person is not meeting the job standards and needs to improve performance.
2. The person is meeting the job standards but still has work to do regarding his behavior.
3. The person has mastered the job, is demonstrating the necessary behaviors, but still needs to learn and develop additional competencies before she is ready for promotion.

▼OUR EXPERIENCE
Dealing with the Four-Letter Word Fear

When we first begin coaching an executive, there is usually a fair amount of fear and anxiety about the exact purpose and reason for the coaching. One executive I coached was so apprehensive during our first meeting that he was going to resign. It took two hours to convince the person that this was not an effort to prove his inadequacy. Quite the contrary. The coaching was intended to further develop his strengths. His fear, however, initially kept him from hearing anything I was saying. There was to be no development until he got over his fear—until he believed that this was a service being provided to him because he was valuable, not because he was defective.

This experience reminded me of my favorite basketball coach in high school. He said to me one day, "Bill, the only time you need to worry is when I stop talking to you. That's when you'll know there is a problem."
—Bill

When most people receive constructive feedback, particularly when it is pointed at one or more of their blind spots, it arouses fear and a host of questions usually goes through their mind—questions which they may or may not verbalize. Questions such as:

- I wonder what this means to my career?
- How long have I been behaving in this way?

- Does everyone agree that I have a problem? Does everyone have a negative opinion of me because of it?
- Just how much improvement and what kind of improvement is my boss looking for?
- How am I going to find time to work on these issues and/or skills when I am so busy getting the job done?
- How am I going to go about improving in these areas?
- What resources are available to me?
- How will I know if I am improving?
- What will be my reward for improving, if any?

These are the questions that should be answered in the process of putting together and presenting a developmental plan to a person.

During the feedback session you want to get as much agreement as you can about what the person's issues are. Sometimes you simply need an intellectual agreement. In other words, you need enough agreement to go forward with your planning. It's common for people to go in and out of denial about their issues. You don't need total buy-in on the issues to proceed with the developmental plan. For example, a person may know he needs work in a certain area but he may not agree about the severity of the problem. He may not fully understand the impact of his behavior.

The exercise of creating a developmental plan with the person in and of itself can help to reduce the person's resistance to owning her strengths and weaknesses which we will talk more about in Chapter 6. The developmental plan should be a plan of hope. It should reduce some of the person's fear of failing. The feedback shows the person the *what*—what it is he needs to change. The developmental plan shows the person the what and the *how*—how is the person going to go about accomplishing the change.

Gaining Commitment

One of the best ways to get the person to buy into her developmental plan and take it seriously is to involve her in the creation of the plan. You may want to rough out the plan in your own mind before you meet with the person, but go through the step-by-step process of creating the actual plan with her. It's hard to argue or fight what one has created. The planning process also provides a context for the feedback you have given her and helps her better understand it's meaning and significance.

If you have successfully engaged the person in the creation of the plan, when you are finished he should be encouraged and hopeful— encouraged about reaching more of his potential and hopeful that he will be able to make the changes outlined in the plan. As you go through the process of developing the plan, you will want to develop a clear vision of how the person will be different. Together you will want to create a picture of what the person will be able to do better, how the person will feel about himself, opportunities that may be available to him as a result of his improvements. The clear vision of the more fulfilled, successful person will serve as an inspiration and motivation, particularly during the dark days when the person is struggling to change and feels he isn't making enough progress.

Primary Issues

The three primary issues you will address in the plan are performance, competencies, and behaviors.

1. *Performance* refers to the person's output. It is the actual results of the person's efforts.
2. *Competencies* refer to the person's skills and abilities. These are the things she can do. A competency actually refers to a grouping of related skills.
3. *Behaviors* relate to the how. How does the person go about achieving the performance results? What are the things he does or doesn't do in achieving the goals and objectives?

Before you begin planning, you should assess what the person's performance level is currently and what it should be. You should assess the competencies she currently has and what competencies she needs for the job. And you should assess the behaviors desired for each competency and which of those behaviors she currently demonstrates. The difference between where she is and where she needs to be as it relates to each of these issues we call gaps. Later in this chapter, we will talk more about assessing the gaps.

Having a clear definition of the competencies and corresponding behaviors required for the position is essential. Figure 5.1 is a sample of some of the managerial competencies and behaviors which have been developed by a company called Exxceed, Inc. (For more information on competency development, you can contact them at the address listed in the Further Reading section in the back of the book.)

However you have defined the required competencies and behaviors, they should have been discussed during the feedback session. In fact, most of the information you will cover in the developmental plan should have already been reviewed during the feedback session. In this step of the process, you are simply putting everything into an organized structure which will help you zero in on what the issues and priorities are.

FIGURE 5.1 Competencies and Behaviors

Task Achievement Competencies	Behaviors
Results Orientation	Sets achievable goals Strives to achieve goals Develops standards against which to measure behavior and performance
Managing Performance	Pays attention to the quality and quantity of performance Sets clear, well-defined desired outcomes for work activity and tracks progress Seeks performance feedback from others
Influence	Develops and presents persuasive arguments to address the concerns, wants, and needs of others Elicits and responds effectively to objections Identifies key decision makers and the people who influence them Anticipates reactions and objections and plans how to overcome them
Initiative	Takes action without being asked or required to do so Initiates individual or group projects and takes complete responsibility for their success
Production Efficiency	Performs tasks efficiently Breaks down projects into component tasks Assigns and utilizes resources effectively, even when scarce

(continued)

FIGURE 5.1 Competencies and Behaviors *(continued)*

Task Achievement Competencies	Behaviors
Flexibility	Promptly switches strategies or tactics if the current ones are not working Operates well in situations when the consequences of decisions and actions are unclear
Innovation	Supports and implements new methods and processes Proactively seeks to test, validate, modify, and improve new ideas or methods to make them as effective as possible
Concerns for Quality	Carefully prepares materials, approaches, and resources Monitors accuracy and quality of other's work and takes action to correct mistakes
Technical Expertise	Has and uses knowledge of basic techniques and concepts Develops technical solutions requiring modifying existing methods, and sometimes creating new methods and techniques
Relationship Competencies	
Teamwork	Fulfills commitments to other team members Provides others with feedback to help them be better team members
Service Orientation	Responds to customer requests in a timely, professional manner Elicits feedback from customers to monitor their satisfaction
Interpersonal Awareness	Listens attentively to people's ideas and concerns Approaches others about sensitive issues in nonthreatening ways
Organizational Savvy	Keeps current on formal and informal communication channels and reporting relationships Develops strategies to gain commitments to projects and strategies based on knowledge of the organization's culture
Relationship Building	Develops rapport easily with a variety of people Modifies communication style to fit the personality and culture of others

(continued)

FIGURE 5.1 Competencies and Behaviors *(continued)*

Relationship Competencies	Behaviors
Conflict Resolution	Expresses disagreements in a way that does not attack or disparage Knows when to compromise and when to take stands
Attention to Communication	Organizes and expresses ideas clearly Creatively identifies and utilizes effective communication methods and channels
Cross-Cultural Sensitivity	Develops a knowledge and understanding of different cultures and backgrounds Modifies communication and behavior based on an understanding of cultural differences
Managerial Competencies	
Building Teamwork	Establishes direction for projects and assignments for team members Helps remove organizational barriers and identifies resources to assist the team
Motivating Others	Promptly recognizes and tackles morale problems Uses a variety of approaches to energize and inspire others
Empowering Others	Allows others to make mistakes and take risks to learn and grow Delegates responsibility to others based on their ability and potential
Developing Others	Provides accurate feedback on individual strengths and weaknesses Helps others examine the barriers to their growth and development

Preparing to Plan

You will need certain information at your fingertips when you are doing the planning. Here's a list of what you will need.

- A copy of the job description (In most companies job descriptions sit on the shelf and are outdated. What is needed is a written description of the person's responsibilities and the authority levels assigned to the job.)

- Current standards and expectations of the job
- Your own expectations of the person
- Job goals, department/team/company goals, and the individual's goals
- The competencies required for the job and the corresponding behaviors expected for each competency
- Notes on the feedback you have given the person (Your own observations, feedback from 360-degree feedback process, and any other feedback, and results of any of the assessments.)
- Mission statement, values, and strategy of the company/organization

This information is essential to providing the structure and context for the plan. As you go about developing the plan, you will want to balance the needs of the person with the needs of the department, team, and company. The idea is to make it as much of a win-win as possible.

Sometimes, as you go through this process, the person will come to his own conclusion that there isn't a fit between what he wants to do and what he is currently doing, or between what he values as a person and what the company values. There may not be a fit between the person's competencies and the competencies needed by the company and where the company is trying to go.

The process of creating a developmental plan poses three basic questions:

1. What do we know about the person?
2. What do we know about the company/team and where it is going?
3. How can we get the person related to the company in the proper way so she can reach her goals while helping the company/team reach its goals?

Steps to Creating the Plan

From the moment you begin creating the plan with the person, it should be a positive experience. The underlying question should not be "How can we fix you?" but "How can we help you achieve more of your potential and realize more of your career goals and aspirations?"

Keep in mind that as we address this issue of developmental planning, we are assuming you have the right person in the job. Here is the basic sequence of steps involved in creating the plan.

Looking toward the Future

- Ask the person what it is she values most in a job and career. What does she feel is her own personal mission in life? Review the company's mission and values and determine if the person and the company fit together.
- Determine where the person is in his career and where he would like to go.
- Review the company's and department/team's strategic plans and the competencies and skills that will be most needed going forward.

Evaluating the Present/Determining the Gaps

- Review the goals, standards, and expectations of the person's current job (performance, competencies, and behaviors).
- Look at the feedback you have given the person and the feedback provided by others, along with the results of any assessment tests.
- Determine the gaps between how the person is performing in her present job and how she should be performing in order to master the job.
- Determine the gaps between the competencies the person currently has and the competencies he needs to master the current job.
- Determine the gaps between the behaviors demonstrated by the person and the behaviors expected of the person in the current job.
- Determine the gaps between the person's current performance, competencies, and behaviors and those required for the next career position/objective.
- Determine the gaps between how the person *perceives* his performance, competencies, and behaviors compared to how you have evaluated them.

Setting Goals

- Set realistic developmental goals in the context of the current job and future career goals.

- Set the priorities by determining the performance, competency, and behavior gaps which are most critical to the person's mastery of the current job.
- Set priorities for her future development (if she is close to mastering the current job) by determining those gaps which are most critical to her longer range career goals.

Developing the Plan

- Develop action steps and timetables for each expected improvement and assign a priority.
- Develop action steps and timetables for each expected improvement needed for the longer-range career goals (if he has mastered enough of the current job to do so).
- Identify resources for each action step.
- Determine methods and timetables for following up and monitoring progress.

Looking toward the Future

The first step in creating a developmental plan is to look toward the future. Where does the person want to go in her career and where is the company/team going? In order for people to commit to their developmental plan they must believe there is something in it for them. The point of self-interest is the best place to begin.

Through our workshops and seminars, particularly for employees, we see many people who have few career aspirations and dreams, or if they have aspirations, they are unfocused. Many of them did have clear dreams at one time, but somewhere along the way they lost them. They got mired down by the responsibilities of life and settled for simply bringing home a paycheck. That's why creating a developmental plan can be so inspiring. With your encouragement and guidance, people can resurrect their career dreams, get excited about reaching more of their potential, and get back in touch with what they truly want in a job and career.

In order for a person to be successful in the turbulent sea of change in which we are all living, he needs a strong boat. On this boat he needs a sail. The sail is his mission—where it is he wants to go. In the same way that the sail enables him to catch the wind that will take him to his destination, his own personal mission is what will enable him to identify and capture the opportunities that come his way.

On the boat he also needs a rudder to guide him. The rudder is his values or what is really important to him in his life and career. His values combined with his mission provide him with the framework for making career choices and decisions. Without these, a person's career is left to chance. He will be at the mercy of the winds of change and will probably end up lost at sea, wondering why he isn't more successful.

Your conversation with the person about his mission and values might go something like this.

Supervisor: Robert, what is it you would really like to do? What is it that is particularly important to you? What makes you happy?

Robert: Well, I really like to make things happen. I have high energy and when I have clearly defined goals like I do here, I thrive on making them happen. I am a strong believer in our product. I believe there is enormous opportunity for our company in this industry which is why we have to move really quickly. It's also why I have so little patience with some of the people on my team who don't seem to have a sense of urgency.

Supervisor: Let's talk about that. Before you came here you worked in a very entrepreneurial environment. Here, of course, everything happens through teams. Relationships are very important. What do you think about that?

Robert: Well, it is different. It takes longer to get things done here. As I said, I am really action oriented. It seems like I have to spend too much time working with the personalities and dynamics involved in getting the job done.

Supervisor: Do you like managing and leading people?

Robert: Sometimes I do but sometimes I find it very frustrating.

Supervisor: What else is important to you in a job? Where do you see yourself down the road? What do you think your real strengths are?

In this conversation, the supervisor is encouraging Robert to really think about what he enjoys doing, what gets him excited. Sometimes people don't perform well, not because they don't have the intellectual firepower to do the job or because they aren't trying, but because there isn't a proper match between what they like to do and what they are doing. In this situation, it appears that Robert has a strong entrepreneurial personality. Getting the job done has a very high value to him but the whole process of getting the work done through others doesn't seem to interest him, so there may be a mismatch between what he values and what is required for the job.

A good exercise is to actually have the person write down her personal mission statement. Ask her what she thinks her talents and gifts are? What do people tell her she is good at? When in her career has she been most successful and most fulfilled? What would her dream job look like? These questions will help her get connected to what she needs in a job in order to unleash her passion. Her passion is what you are after because it is essential to high performance.

Evaluating the Present/Determining the Gaps

After you look at where the person wants to go in his career in the context of where the company/team is going, you will want to turn your attention to the present. You are looking at what you know about his current performance. You will want to look at the feedback you have already given him about his performance, which should have included a summary of the 360-degree feedback and any other feedback you may have received, and the results of any assessments he may have taken.

Developmental planning is all about narrowing the gaps. Identifying the gaps is critical because the gaps are where the opportunities for growth lie. You should do three types of gap analysis: 1) a gap analysis for the current job, 2) a gap analysis for the person's career objective/next position, and 3) a perceptual gap analysis. A gap analysis shows the distance between where the person currently is and where she needs to be. Following is an explanation of each.

Gap Analysis for Current Job

In this analysis, you are evaluating the person's level of functioning in his current job compared to how he should be functioning in the job. To effectively complete this analysis, you should have clearly defined the performance expectations, competencies, and behaviors required for the job. Figure 5.2 presents a rating system and Figure 5.3 shows a sample grid which can help you in your analysis.

FIGURE 5.2 Rating System

Performance: How well is the person performing in the job compared to the standards and expectations set for the job and person?

1. Does not meet standards at all
2. Meets most standards
3. Meets all standards

Competencies: What kinds of competencies does the person have compared to the competencies that are required to perform successfully in the job?

1. Needs work on one or more competencies
2. Has most competencies needed for job
3. Has all the needed competencies

Behaviors: What kinds of behaviors does the person demonstrate compared to the behaviors required of the job?

1. Needs to improve one or more behaviors
2. Demonstrates most behaviors
3. Demonstrates all of the needed behaviors

FIGURE 5.3 Gap Analysis for Current Job

	Standard Being Met	Job/Organizational Standard	Gap
Performance	3	3	0
Competencies	1	3	2
Behaviors	1	3	2

In the sample grid in Figure 5.3 you can see from the ratings that the person is meeting the job standards but needs work on some of his competencies and behaviors. The person is getting to the results but needs work on how he is going about achieving them. A rating of 3 is the organizational standard. Anything less than that represents a gap.

Gap Analysis for Career Objective/Next Position

In this analysis you are evaluating where the person currently is in the mastery of her job compared to how she will need to perform if she were promoted to the next position. You will only want to consider the future position or career goal if the person has mastered a good part of the current job. Unfortunately, sometimes people want to work on preparing themselves for the next position before they have mastered the one they are in. To complete the grid in Figure 5.5 you should have already identified the competencies and behaviors required for their next career position or their career objectives based on the rating system in Figure 5.4.

As with the grid in Figure 5.3, the organizational standard is 3. As you can see from the grid in Figure 5.5, the person has large gaps in competencies and behaviors. This means that the person has a lot of work to do before she would be ready to take on the next position. It shows that she would have some difficulty meeting the performance standards at this point.

FIGURE 5.4 Rating System

Performance: How well is the person performing in the current job compared to where the person would need to be in order to be promoted to the next position?

1. A long way to go
2. Almost there
3. Ready for promotion now

Competencies: What competencies does the person have now compared to the competencies required for the next position?

1. Needs many more competencies
2. Needs a few more competencies
3. Has all that are needed for the next position

Behaviors: What behaviors is the person currently demonstrating compared to the behaviors expected in the next position?

1. Needs to demonstrate many more behaviors
2. Demonstrates most of the behaviors
3. Demonstrates all of the behaviors needed for the next position

FIGURE 5.5 Gap Analysis for Career Objective/Next Position

	Standard Being Met	Job/Organizational Standard	Gap
Performance	2	3	1
Competencies	1	3	2
Behaviors	1	3	2

Perceptual Gap Analysis

This analysis shows how the person perceives himself compared to how you have evaluated him. How you evaluate/perceive him may or may not be different from how he perceives himself. Assuming you have provided an accurate, objective evaluation that is close to reality (there will always be an element of subjectivity so you can never be sure your picture of reality is totally correct), the difference between your evaluation of the person and his perception of himself reveals the distance he has to travel to master the current job and achieve his next career objective. The difference also reveals his blind spots—the things about himself he cannot see. Getting him to *believe* that he needs to change and getting him to actually change are two different things.

You may not want to go through the perceptual gap analysis with the person but instead use it for your own purposes as an internal guide. The perceptual gap analysis helps you understand the work you have to do in helping him own his blind spots. Completing the perceptual gap analysis together in some cases could create more resistance on the part of the person. Dealing with resistance requires a fair amount of subtlety and diplomacy. Figure 5.6 gives the rating system you could use for perceptual gap analysis.

FIGURE 5.6 Rating System

> **Performance:** How does the person's perception of performance in the current job compare to how the manager believes the person is performing?
>
> 1. Is not meeting standards
> 2. Is meeting standards
> 3. Is exceeding standards
>
> **Competencies:** How does the person's perception of competencies compare to how the manager views the person's competencies?
>
> 1. Needs work on one or more competencies
> 2. Has the necessary competencies
> 3. Competencies exceed those needed for the job
>
> **Behaviors:** How does the person's perception of demonstrated behavior compare to how the manager perceives the person's behaviors?
>
> 1. Needs to improve one or more behaviors
> 2. Demonstrates most behaviors
> 3. Demonstrates all of the needed behaviors

FIGURE 5.7 Perceptual Gap Analysis

	Person's Perception	Manager's Evaluation	Gap
Performance	3	3	0
Competencies	2	1	1
Behaviors	2	1	1

The grid in Figure 5.7 reveals that the manager and the person have a gap in how they view his competencies and behaviors. The person believes he has all of the necessary competencies and demonstrates most of the necessary behaviors, while the manager believes the person needs work on one or more competencies and needs to improve one or more behaviors. If the manager is perceiving the person correctly, the person has some blind spots.

Based on the grids in Figures 5.3, 5.5, and 5.7, here is an excerpt of a conversation between a manager and his direct report as they discuss the gaps. We will continue the conversation with Robert from page 97.

Supervisor: Robert, let's recap our earlier feedback session and try to zero in on what your developmental priorities should be. We talked about the fact that in terms of results you are getting the job done. You are accomplishing the work goals that we established together. (Recap results.) As I mentioned, I am very pleased with your results. (Pause.) However, we need to do some work on process—how you go about getting those results.

We agreed that you need to work on some of your relationship competencies and managerial competencies. We agreed that you can improve the performance of your team by giving them more feedback, both individually and as a team. We also talked about how you can improve your interpersonal skills by listening better and dealing more effectively with conflict. We mentioned that you can work on being more sensitive to others by watching and listening to cues better. Have you thought some more about these issues since our feedback session?

Robert: Yes, I agree with most of them but the one that is still bothering me is the whole sensitivity issue. When you said I'm sometimes overly aggressive and that people perceive me as being insensitive to their needs, that really upset me because I don't see myself that way. Sure, I push for results, but I think every good manager has to do that if he is going to get the job done.

Supervisor: I understand your concern. None of us likes to hear that we are coming across in a way that we do not intend. I'm sure you don't mean to be insensitive and I know you are very conscientious about getting the job done. I appreciate that, but we need to make sure that you aren't damaging some of your relationships in the process. Those relationships must be preserved if you are going to get the job done long range. In our work together, we need to try to understand better how some of these perceptions are being formed. What are some of the things you are saying and doing to cause people to feel the way they do? Are you aware your people are afraid of you? Do you know they are withholding information from you because of their fears?

Robert: Well, you told me that in our feedback session, but I still think that if they were doing their jobs I wouldn't have to come down hard on them. People just don't seem to want to work hard today.

Supervisor: Robert, I think we are getting off the point. We aren't talking about other people. We are talking about you and your behavior. I have seen how you put fear in people. The other day as I was walking by your office I heard you say something forcibly to one of your staff members. You said, "Now, you better get with it." Your 360-degree feedback confirmed the same thing. This was not an isolated occurrence. You may not intend to put fear in people, but it's a fact that people feel that way. We need to come up with some things you can do behaviorally to change some of these dynamics and perceptions. Are you willing to explore that with me?

Robert: Okay.

Supervisor: I think one of the reasons you are struggling with some of your relationships with your people is because of some management issues. When management principles are not followed, problems often degenerate into personality conflicts. In the 360-degree feedback process, some of your people commented that they are unclear about what their responsibilities are and that they feel they don't have enough decision-making authority. They feel that too many things have to go through you. So those are some areas we need to address as well. Have you thought about these issues?

Robert: Yes, as a matter of fact I have. I just don't feel that I should have to spell everything out for people. When you are running as fast and hard as we are, you don't always have time to detail exactly what people are supposed to do. The mission of our team is very clear and so is the work that has to be done. As far as decision making goes, I really don't feel I can trust them with some decisions yet. Some of the times I have trusted them and given them the decision making, they didn't use it wisely and we all got burned.

Supervisor: On your first point, people do need to work with more ambiguity today but you can help to remove some of that ambiguity by making people's roles very clear. If you don't, people will spend their time trying to figure out what they are supposed to do instead of focusing on getting the job done. I would like you to make sure that you don't have any duplication in responsibilities or that any responsibilities are going unattended because the expectations of each person were unclear. As far as the decision making goes, maybe you need to spend more time coaching and training your people if you don't feel they are capable of making decisions. Or maybe you don't have the right people in the jobs. In either situation, you need to find a way to delegate more decision making so that you can be freed up to be creative and make more strategic decisions.

Robert: Okay, I can work on that.

Supervisor: I know you are interested in moving on to the next position which is that of vice president. In addition to the things we just mentioned, you also need to work on some of your leadership competencies before you are ready for promotion.

Robert: Well, I'm not sure I agree. I think I am ready for the next position now. In the ten years that I have been with this company, I have consistently produced results. I have never failed on one of my objectives. I don't know many people who can say the same.

Supervisor: You are right, Robert. You have produced some amazing results. The next position requires a very different skill set—skills that will make or break you. The further up you go, the more your success will depend on how well you are able to interact with others—those above you and below you. We can work on some of those competencies now in the context of your current job, but I think our main focus right now should be on mastering your current job. Why don't we set another date to talk about developing more leadership competencies?

As you can see from this sample conversation, the manager is recapping the highlights of the feedback session which should flow right into the statement of some clear objectives and an action plan. This conversation about Robert's gaps also allows the manager to see how well Robert has received and digested the feedback he was given earlier. Your meetings with your people might not go quite as smoothly as this hypothetical conversation. If there are some rough spots in the conversation, don't take it personally and don't assume you haven't done your job. Resist the temptation to tell people what they want to hear just so they will like you.

Setting Goals

We once worked in a company that had established developmental plans for each individual but the plans never made mention of any developmental goals. There were plenty of action steps but no goals. Nobody knew where the action steps were leading or when they had achieved success because they had no way of measuring their progress, no concrete goals toward which to strive.

When you set developmental goals for people, make sure you don't set too many goals and make sure the goals are attainable. As we have said before, people change in small increments. If the developmental goals are too ambitious, you will set the person up for failure. You especially want the person to have some successes early on. This entire process is intended to get people excited about their own development which is why they need to experience some early successes.

You may have covered a lot of ground in your feedback session but the goals or priorities should not number more than two or three. They should be very focused and specific. Think of how difficult it is to change the smallest habits. If you give them too many things to work on at once, they will become overwhelmed and focus on nothing.

Here are four questions you will want to ask yourself to determine if you have set the right developmental goals:

1. Is the accomplishment of each of these goals critical to the person's success in the current job or a requirement for being promoted to the next job?
2. What could be the consequences if the person does not accomplish each of these developmental goals?
3. Are there any other changes that the person must make in order to meet the job standards and/or get promoted? If so, what?
4. Do the goals communicate clearly to the person what the new performance should look like?

Your conversation about the goals might go something like this:

Supervisor: Robert, we have covered a lot of ground. Let's try to bottom line what we have talked about and create some concrete goals. Based on what we have said, the areas you need to work on most are your interpersonal skills and management skills. How can we turn these into specific goals?

From here you would establish the goals. The goals might look something like this:

- To develop stronger, more trusting relationships with the people I manage by having more direct, constructive communication with them
- To deal more effectively with conflict by working through it with people instead of avoiding it
- To improve my management effectiveness by better defining responsibilities, delegating more, and following up

Developing the Plan

As you can see from the thought process we have gone through in this chapter, getting to a simple plan requires a fair amount of thought and analysis. It also requires some influencing skills to get the person to participate in its development and buy in to what the two of you have created. The process isn't quite as complicated as it may look, however.

The entire formula we have provided for creating a developmental plan doesn't have to be committed to writing. The written plan should consist of the vision, the developmental goals and objectives, the action steps and timetables for accomplishing the objectives, the resources available to the person, and how his progress will be monitored. All of the thinking leading up to the plan, however, does not need to be committed to writing. The whole idea is to get at what is important to the person's success and the team/company's success.

Once you have identified the priorities or objectives, you'll want to develop some action steps. The action steps should be concrete and specific and should provide for daily actions. The conscious daily focus on the priorities and the taking of small steps every day, even if just for a few minutes, is where the most significant change usually comes from. Books, training programs, and seminars are fine but they don't allow for enough practice and application.

The plan should identify the resources for each action step. It should also explain how the person will get feedback and how progress will be monitored. We will talk more about that in Chapter 6. The plan should be flexible enough to allow for changing circumstances and for changing competency levels. Here's a continuation of the supervisor's conversation with Robert.

Supervisor: Now that we know what the priorities are, let's put together some action steps for addressing each one. These action steps can include a whole host of activities, including observation of others, personal interviews with people, classes, books, role playing during coaching sessions, on-the-job spot coaching, reflection, and analyzing real-world experiences with me. What do you think are some action steps you can take for the first goal: developing more trusting relationships with your people by having more direct, constructive communication with them?

Together, you and the person can brainstorm ideas. Figure 5.8 shows what the plan for that priority might look like. These may seem like too many action steps to concentrate on, but most of these items are interrelated with building trust through better communication as the focus. In Chapter 6, we will talk more about how you can help people work on their action steps on a day-to-day basis.

FIGURE 5.8 Action Plan

Priority: To develop stronger, more trusting relationships with the people I manage by having more direct, constructive communication with them

Action Steps

Hold staff meetings weekly

Meet with direct reports individually every Monday morning

Hold formal coaching sessions at least quarterly with each direct report

Control my temper and apologize if it comes out

Practice listening more and saying less

Issue fewer orders and ask more questions as a way of leading people to their own answers

Request feedback frequently from direct reports

Identify and observe leaders in the company who are good at communicating with their people

Take a course on interpersonal skills

Revising the Plan

The developmental plan should not be fixed in stone. It is simply a guide for helping people grow and develop. In order for it to be a viable tool for growth, the plan should be constantly changing. The plan should be revised whenever one or more of the following occurs:

- The person has mastered one or more of the goals and needs new challenges.
- An action step recommended in the plan isn't working and a new one is needed to replace it.
- Changes in the person's job require that she have a different set of competencies.
- New needs surface as a result of the coaching process.
- The person's performance changes significantly, either positively or negtively.

Developmental Plan Checklist

Here's a quick checklist which will help you evaluate how well you have done the developmental planning.

1. Did you give the person time to think about and digest the feedback you gave him before putting together the developmental plan?
   Yes ☐   No ☐

2. Did you involve the person in creating the plan?
   Yes ☐   No ☐

3. Did you go about the planning process in your own mind before involving the person?
   Yes ☐   No ☐

4. Did you and the person develop a clear vision of where she would be when she accomplished the objectives in the plan?
   Yes ☐   No ☐

5. Was the person motivated by the plan and excited about working on his development when you finished it?
   Yes ☐   No ☐

6. Did you help her gain clarity about what is important to her and where she wants to go with her career?
   Yes ☐   No ☐

7. Did you look at the team/company's needs and where it's going and examine the fit with the person's needs and objectives?
   Yes ☐   No ☐

8. Did you review the feedback you have already given him as well as the expectations of the job?
   Yes ☐   No ☐

9. Did you do a gap analysis of her performance, competencies, and behaviors in relation to the current job and, if appropriate, the next position to which she is aspiring?
   Yes ☐ No ☐

10. Did you do a perceptual gap analysis as a way of determining how much work you need to do in working with his resistance? (Assuming your perceptions are correct.)
    Yes ☐ No ☐

11. Did you set realistic developmental goals which are critical to her performance in her current position and/or her future position?
    Yes ☐ No ☐

12. Did you limit the goals to two or three and did you identify specific action steps for each?
    Yes ☐ No ☐

13. Did you identify the resources available to the person?
    Yes ☐ No ☐

14. Does the plan describe how the person will get feedback and how his progress will be monitored?
    Yes ☐ No ☐

15. Is the plan flexible enough to allow for changing circumstances and competency levels?
    Yes ☐ No ☐

Evaluation: Every task listed above is essential to creating and using a developmental plan which does in fact improve behavior and performance and help the person grow. In summary, the plan must be created in the context of the company's goals, the team's goals, and the person's career goals. The person must participate in the creation of the plan. The plan must be committed to writing and referred to frequently if the developmental goals are going to be accomplished. The plan is the person's road map to success.

PERSONAL APPLICATION CORNER

Have you ever had a relationship in which you were having some difficulty, but after much discussion and work, you arrived at a better understanding of one another? You had a breakthrough of sorts. But not long after were you right back in the same old soup? Were you left wondering what happened?

What probably happened was you failed to develop a specific plan for how you were going to improve the relationship or resolve the problem. Agreeing on the problem is one thing; taking concrete steps to do something about it is another.

Something to Try: Think about the personal relationship you have been working on. Hopefully, through your dialogue you are coming to a better understanding of one another. Take one aspect of your relationship or one issue you are working on with the other person and together address the following:

- What is the issue? (Try to pick only one.)
- What is our shared objective as it relates to this issue?
- What are some specific things each of us can do each day or regularly to accomplish this objective?
- How long a time period will we give ourselves to practice these new behaviors before we evaluate our progress?
- What kind of rules should we have for giving each other feedback?

Make sure you commit your ideas to paper so you can refer to what you agreed to regularly. The written plan will help you stay focused and committed. It will also serve as the basis for evaluating your progress.

CHAPTER SIX

STEP 4

Break through Resistance

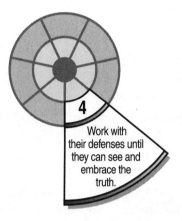

4

Work with their defenses until they can see and embrace the truth.

When you stick with people until they feel safe enough to admit to and own their weaknesses, you empower them to create positive changes in their lives and careers which builds trust.

Have you ever had someone deliver some less than complimentary news to you about some aspect of your behavior or personality—news that just didn't seem to fit your own view of yourself? How did you react? Did you react with curiosity and interest? Did you objectively try to understand what you may have done or said to cause the person to give you such feedback? Or did you become upset and immediately start defending yourself? Worse yet, did you go on the attack?

How about the reverse? Have you ever given one of your people feedback about some aspect of her performance which needed improvement only to have her turn on you as though you were the enemy? If either of these situations is familiar, you have experienced what is called *resistance*. In the first scenario, your own, and in the latter, someone else's.

In Chapter 1, we defined coaching as the process of developing a relationship and environment through which people can discover their greatness, deal with their deficiencies and dark sides, reach more of their potential, and accomplish their objectives. When we talk about deficiencies and dark sides, we are referring to those things which are keeping the person from performing up to the job standard.

A deficiency can be something as simple as a skill the person has yet to master—a skill which is necessary to the successful accomplishment of the job, such as effective presentation skills or organizational skills. When we refer to the person's dark side, we aren't necessarily referring to some evil, sinister side of a person but more to those things which the person cannot see about himself—those things which are keeping him from being as effective as he could be.

A dark side of a person, for example, could be a person's tendency to become condescending and insensitive to the feelings of others when she has an important job to do and is under a lot of pressure. Helping people see and own their dark sides, their blind spots, in a way that liberates them is one of the most challenging parts of the coaching process. It's also where the real gold is—the greatest opportunity for growth. What people can't see about themselves, both positive and negative, can hurt them tremendously. Breaking through people's resistance to seeing and owning their weaknesses and sometimes even their strengths requires real skill and patience. It cannot be done by force. It is a softening process in which the person no longer sees the need to protect himself from the truth about some aspect of himself.

Sometimes, in the course of coaching an executive, we discover that the person's boss has a real dark side which manifests itself as an unwillingness to change herself. When this happens, rarely is there a change in the executive we are coaching. In most cases, the boss needs to change almost as much as the individual. The boss must demonstrate a willingness to meet some of the individual's expectations and must respond to the person's needs. The boss is key to breaking through the person's resistance. One of the best ways to do that is by having a healthy give and take.

We once coached a fairly high-level executive who had 22 people reporting to him. He felt his job was so important that he had to remain consistently strong, which to him meant showing no openness and always sticking to his original thoughts and plans. He never admitted he was wrong and he never changed in response to his people. The result was that any time he asked his people to change, it was met with great resistance. He got back the exact same behavior he was demonstrating.

▼OUR EXPERIENCE

Reality Check

I coached the president of a corporation once who repeatedly told me how honest he was with everyone. The story I got from the troops was radically different, to say the least. Not open, untrustworthy, lacking in integrity were terms they used to describe him. They saw him as anything but honest.

First, I helped him get clarity on what the true picture was and then I taught him how to tell the truth about what was happening in the company and how to tell people the truth about their performance. Over time, the truth eventually did set him free and people began to trust him.

Every time we withhold or twist the truth, we destroy trust. Every time we tell people the truth, even if it is news they don't want to hear, we build trust. This particular executive went on to be one of the best leaders in the company once he learned the importance of being straight with people.

—Bill

Self-Esteem Is the Issue

Most of the executives we coach in our day-to-day coaching practice are highly intelligent, overachievers with an impressive track record. Whether we are doing developmental coaching (which is most of the work we do) or fix-them-or-they're-gone coaching, we are usually met with a fair amount of resistance in the beginning—resistance which must be dealt with if there is to be any significant change.

Sometimes we come across a person who is already aware of her weaknesses and is willing to work on them. She isn't shocked by the constructive criticism we give her upon completion of the 360-degree interviews and psychological and performance assessments. And then there is the rare exception who is unaware of his weaknesses but who also doesn't try to defend himself when he receives negative feedback. Instead, he looks at it as an opportunity to learn about himself and grow as a person.

The majority of people are hearing the constructive feedback we give them for the first time. Many have been working and succeeding in their careers for years and no one has ever given them any straight talk about their strengths and weaknesses until now.

Some are confused and baffled. If some aspect of their behavior has been a problem, why hasn't someone told them before now? Good question.

Particularly for type A, high achievers who usually set high standards for themselves, hearing that they are not perfect is often a blow to their self-esteem. If they are overly identified with their jobs, meaning their whole self-worth is wrapped up in their work, any kind of negative feedback can be devastating. Or if the person has a poor sense of self-esteem to begin with, any bad news is just reinforcement of the secretly held negative beliefs she holds about herself.

Whenever someone reacts very strongly to negative feedback it is usually for one of two reasons. Either the feedback is in fact off base and unjustified (which is why your feedback should always be grounded in fact) or his sense of self-esteem is being threatened. If you find yourself in a heated debate with a person about what you are telling her and you are going back and forth about details and issues, remember the real issue on the table is her self-worth—not the points you are debating.

As we have said previously, if we all had a perfectly healthy sense of self-esteem, none of this would be a problem. There would be no resistance. We could hear the other person without getting defensive because our self-esteem is not dependent upon the opinions of others and we would know that we are much more than whatever weaknesses we and others might uncover about ourselves. It doesn't mean we believe everything we are told, but we are open to looking at ourselves objectively.

OUR EXPERIENCE

Success Does not Equal Self-Esteem

One of my most challenging coaching assignments was with an executive who was earning well over a seven-figure salary at a well-known Fortune 100 company. He obviously had an impressive career track record, but he had some issues that needed addressing. Together we had defined some very clear developmental goals to work on during our coaching sessions.

Every time we met for a coaching session, after I inquired about what was new, I would ask him in a nonthreatening way how he was doing with the issues we had identified in his developmental plan. Every time his response was the same, "Oh, that's not a problem." Or he would change the subject. Most people, once they stop resisting and admit, "Yes, this is me," take a kind of pride in recounting their successes and their slips—the times when they caught themselves falling back into their old behaviors—at each session. But not this person. According to him, he had no issues.

Finally, after trying everything I could to work with his resistance, I said to him, "You know, I don't think you need me anymore because

every time we get anywhere close to one of the issues we identified in
your developmental plan, you say it's not a problem or you change the
subject. I feel like I keep running up against a brick wall."

His response astonished me. He said, "Every time you leave here I feel
like a failure—like I can't do anything right." He continued to say, "You
don't know what it is like working here. The pressure is beyond belief. I
don't have some of the credentials or background that some of my col-
leagues have and I often don't feel confident."

One would think that a person who had achieved the level he had
would know his worth. I was impressed by what he had achieved and I
saw him as an authentic, gutsy, capable person. I didn't see the need to
constantly stroke him but that is exactly what he needed—more so than
most. The challenge for me was to step back, take it slow, reinforce his
positive qualities, and make it safe for him to admit his weaknesses.
—Diane

Compassionate Coaching

There is one quality that every coach must have if he is going to succeed at helping people be their best and that is compassion. Compassion is the healing balm that takes the sting out of looking at parts of
ourselves that we don't want to look at. Compassion is what allows the
negative feedback to heal us rather than inflict yet another wound. It's
the safety net when we feel embarrassed and vulnerable in the presence
of another human being who has seen a side of us that we have secretly
tried to keep hidden from other people and sometimes even ourselves.

There is a wonderful quote which speaks to the issue of compassion:
"If we could read the secret history of our enemies, we should find in
each man's life sorrow and suffering enough to drain all hostility." This
is a good quote to remember when you are coaching a person who becomes angry and belligerent when you are giving her negative feedback.

Research studies have revealed that by the time most people reach
adulthood, they have received on average a ratio of 18 negative comments about themselves to each positive one. Most of us don't want
to hear one more time how we are defective unless we can see some
good coming from it. Usually, those people who are the most defensive
and difficult to deal with are the ones whose self-esteem has been the
most injured.

One of the rewards of our coaching practice is the feeling that we are truly assisting people. If nothing else, we provide them a safe place where they can be themselves and speak openly about what they think and feel without the fear that they will be judged or penalized in some way. Although our work is not therapy, it's amazing what some of these highly successful, together-looking executives reveal about themselves in the course of our coaching sessions.

Once we were coaching an executive who was very successful in his career but when he was under stress he would often forget the people around him. They became tools for getting the job done. His body language would change, his tone of voice became very serious and stern. People saw him as overly aggressive and driven. In the course of our coaching, he revealed that in his nine years of college (he had a Ph.D.) he never achieved less than a 3.9 average. In high school, he was the captain of the football team and the baseball team. His list of achievements throughout his life was truly remarkable.

One day in conversation, he mentioned that when he was growing up the pressure to achieve was almost unbearable. If he ever came home with less than 100 percent or straight As there was always a huge price to pay. Is there any small wonder that when this person was under stress he exhibited the behaviors he did? In his mind, achievement of the task or goal was everything. It's what he had gotten rewarded for all his life (until now) and failure of any kind was what he had gotten severely chastised for.

If we knew people's history, probably none of their behaviors would look strange to us. It would make perfect sense given where each had come from. Again, as a coach or manager it isn't our job to delve into a person's past but it is our job to believe in them as people. It's our job to understand that behind the facade of success which most of us try to project, there is a person who is struggling. There are a few rare souls out there who have it together, but most people are still struggling with self-esteem issues and are searching for answers.

Signs of Resistance

People display their resistance or defensiveness in a variety of ways. Have you ever coached a person who suddenly became mute when you got to the constructive criticism? With folded arms, the person either wouldn't look at you at all or stared at you with a glazed look on her face, refusing to engage in any kind of conversation.

Or maybe you have found yourself in a coaching session where all of a sudden you are on a different subject than the one you wanted to address—namely how the person needs to improve. Switching the focus to someone else or something else is one of the most common ways employees resist hearing what you are telling them.

And then there are those who become downright nasty. The best defense is a good offense, so they go on the attack. The other extreme is what we call passive-aggressive—the person who smiles and nods his head in agreement but doesn't believe a word you are saying. You may think all is well, but if you could hear his conversation to others once he leaves your office you would be shocked.

Here's a list of just some of the behaviors that people exhibit when they feel they need to defend themselves against what you are saying:

- Taking offense
- Loss of humor
- Needing to be right
- Rise in volume of voice
- Flooding with information to prove a point
- Endless explaining and rationalizing
- "Poor me"
- Teaching or preaching
- Rigidity
- Denying
- Withdrawing into deadly silence
- Cynicism
- Sarcasm
- Being highly critical
- Terminal uniqueness
- "That's just how I am"
- Refusing to negotiate
- Blaming
- Suddenly tired, sleepy, or sick
- Intellectualizing
- Being too nice
- Selective deafness

- Attacking
- Holding a grudge
- Trivializing with humor
- Inappropriate laughter or giggling
- Sour grapes
- Sidetracking the conversation
- Overdramatizing
- Negative facial expressions and closed body language

Learning to identify these defense mechanisms when they occur is the first step to breaking through the resistance. The challenge is not to take any of it personally so that it interferes with your feedback. If you do, you will lose your objectivity and you will not be in a position to help the person. That doesn't mean you let the person walk all over you and abuse you, but it means you know the problem is about her, not you. (That's provided you are following the process correctly).

Techniques for Reducing Resistance

Think of the resistance as a brick wall which is keeping the person from hearing and embracing what you are mirroring to them. If you try to remove this wall with a sledgehammer or grenade, the resistance will only get stronger. The secret is to work with it creatively in a way that the person sees that he is hurting himself by keeping it intact. You also have to make it safe for him to let the wall down. The following are some examples of ways you can do that.

Keep Presenting the Facts

When you see a person is not buying what you are saying, you want to stay centered and keep feeding her facts and information about her behavior and performance in an objective way. Do not judge or criticize because it will only make her more defensive. Stay away from comments like, "See, that's exactly what I am talking about. You are so closed minded." Avoid using words like stupid, lame brain, and idiotic—whether in reference to her or something she said. Simply state the facts and keep restating them until she is forced to look at them. Sometimes you may feel like a broken record. That's okay. Like a mirror, you just keep reflecting back what you see.

Consistency is the key here. We once coached a woman who kept her people in a state of terror because she was constantly changing the facts as she saw them regarding their performance. One minute they felt like superstars and the next minute they thought they would be out the door soon. People need clear, centered, consistent feedback about their strengths and weaknesses if they are going to change.

Affirm Their Strengths

When a person gets emotional, he often loses perspective and reads into things the other person is saying. He writes his own story—often an incorrect one—around what you are saying. With people who are very sensitive or who have a low sense of self-esteem, you will want to keep giving them the balanced picture—the positive and the negative at the same time. You may have to tell them what you are *not* saying about them and their performance when you give constructive feedback.

Look for Real-Time Demonstrations of Behaviors

If a person continues to deny that she acts or behaves in a certain way on the job, look to see if she demonstrates those very behaviors while you are meeting with her. For example, once we coached a woman who would not stop talking. We would ask her a question and by the time she finished her long-winded response we couldn't remember what the question was. She would cover every little detail and tangent that was re-motely related to the question. When she did so in the course of our coaching sessions, we would stop her and ask her to look at what she just did. She began to see her pattern and responded positively by speaking less and sticking to the point.

If a person, for example, is not cooperating with others on the job and you are trying to get him to see and own up to that part of himself, look to see if he demonstrates such qualities while you are talking to him about the issue. If he talks over you or is totally closed-minded— whatever the dysfunctional behavior, use it as an example of the point you are trying to get across. The more immediate you are with the feed-back, the better.

Show Vulnerability Yourself

When people are acting defensively they are usually afraid of the information you are presenting to them. They are afraid of being seen for who they are and being judged harshly. If you see a person struggling with what you are telling her, sometimes it's a good idea to share with her a personal experience you had when you were in a similar position, a time when you received some feedback about yourself which was devastating.

You may or may not want to tell people what your issue was but you do want to tell them how you felt. Then you want to encourage them by telling them how much you benefited from the information once you got over the feelings. What you are doing is giving people permission to be human, something many of them can't give to themselves. By telling your own story, you are saying to them: "We all mess up. None of us is perfect. Because we have some weaknesses doesn't mean all is lost or that we are defective human beings." When you tell people your story don't make it one way. Encourage them to talk about their feelings.

Communicate Rewards and/or Consequences

There has to be some reason for people to go through the discomfort of looking at their weaknesses. Give them some incentive, some vision of the good that can come to them if they make the changes you are requesting. You might say, for example: "John, you have a lot of potential at this company but you aren't living up to it because of the way you sometimes treat other people. I know you want to be promoted to a supervisor and I am willing to work with you to help you accomplish that goal but first we have to look at this issue." In other words, put the issue in the context of something the person wants.

If people continue to resist after you've done everything you can to get them to look at their issues, sometimes the best response is to say something like: "Mary, we've talked a lot about this issue. I want to help you but you discount the feedback I have given you. It doesn't appear that you are hearing me. You don't have to agree, but there are some behavior changes which I expect you to make." And then you proceed to be specific about what those behavior changes should be.

Here's a situation in which a manager is trying to get an employee named Sara to own up to the fact that she is consistently late in submitting her work. The manager has set the stage for the coaching session and is now in the middle of giving Sara feedback.

Manager: Sara, your work has been consistently late during the last six months. You've missed a number of deadlines which has affected the performance of the entire team. What do you think that is about?

Sara: I think you are exaggerating. Maybe I've been late a few times but I am usually on time. Besides, I have a heavier workload than most of my peers in the department.

Manager: It has been more than a few times, Sara. I have samples of your work right here, the dates they were due, and the dates you submitted them.

Sara: Well, a couple of those assignments were interrupted because of other work you gave me. Some of the other assignments didn't seem that critical to me. I don't understand what the big deal is. I have been a loyal employee in this department for five years. I miss a few deadlines and you make me feel like a school girl being reprimanded for turning papers in late.

Manager: Sara, you have been a loyal employee for the last five years. You do excellent work and I can count on you to be a team player. I guess that's why I am concerned. I'm wondering why there has been a change in the last six months. Your work always used to be on time. Some of the deadlines you have missed have been very important ones which affected almost everyone in the department. (Cite examples.) So, why are you having difficulty now? What can I do to help you? (Sara begins to cry.) Sara, why are you crying? What's going on? (Manager allows for silence.)

Sara: I know I have been late with my work. It's just that my life seems to be falling apart and I am having trouble concentrating. It looks like my husband wants a divorce but the worst part is he is threatening to get custody of my children. Every day almost I am on the phone with my lawyer, my relatives—it's just a mess. I am so scared and upset most days I can't even think straight.

Manager: I am very sorry to hear that, Sara. It sounds like you are going through a very difficult time. I understand better now. Maybe if you had told me sooner that you were experiencing personal problems

I could have helped in some way. I know you are going through a difficult time, Sara, but we still need to find a way to meet the deadlines. Let's see what we can figure out together.

Sara: Okay. Thanks for understanding.

Manager: Well, first of all, are you seeing a counsellor—someone who can help you deal with what you are feeling?

Sara: No, not really. Just a few girlfriends.

Manager: Why don't you call the number for our employee assistance program? It's all confidential and they have trained professionals who can be very helpful. I think you could really benefit from using that service, at least until things start to settle down for you.

Sara: Maybe I will.

Manager: One thing we will do is sit down every Monday morning to review your workload and what your week looks like. Maybe we can lighten your workload a little bit until you get some of these problems ironed out. The other thing I would like you to do is to let me know the minute you think you won't meet a deadline. Don't wait until the day something is due to tell me. Okay?

Sara: Sure.

Manager. What about all the telephone calls? Are they all necessary? Could you make whatever phone calls you *have* to make at a certain time each day and refuse to take some calls? Maybe this will keep you from staying stirred up throughout the day. What do you think?

Sara: Maybe so. I'll try it.

Manager: What else can I do to help you, Sara?

Sara: Nothing I can think of. Thank you so much for understanding.

Manager: You're welcome, Sara. I hope things get better for you soon. We'll meet next Monday to review your workload but why don't we plan to meet two weeks from now to see how things are going.

Sara: Okay.

In this situation, the manager did not assume that Sara was just lazy and didn't care. He did not demand that she clean up her act and start submitting work on time which would have only made Sara more resistant. In this instance, Sara needed understanding, not judgment. The manager tried to find out why her work was suffering. Because the manager was understanding, Sara finally felt safe enough to stop minimizing and denying the problem and talk about the real reasons why she was having difficulty.

Sticking with It

We said that coaching takes compassion but it also takes an enormous amount of patience. When you are met with resistance which appears to be mounting into a conflict, the temptation is to avoid it, to cut it off. We do that in a variety of ways. Have you ever tried the positive approach with a difficult employee only to get so frustrated that you decided to put an end to the discomfort you were feeling? Maybe you said something to the effect of: "Look, I've been trying to help you but you aren't cooperating so now I am going to get tough. I'm the boss so just do as I say." You play the power card.

You may not have said those exact words but that's the message you send when you are unable to live in what is called the tension of the opposites. The tension of the opposites occurs when one person sees things one way and the other person sees it a different way. The challenge is to stay in the tension, keep processing your thoughts and ideas together in an honest, genuine way until someone has a breakthrough; until you have come to some agreement.

Many people have difficulty living in the tension of the opposites because they are afraid of conflict. Conflict to them means something bad is going to happen. Actually, when we refuse to engage in healthy conflict—which is what living in the tension of the opposites is about—the problem or disagreement is never solved. The problem or issue keeps resurfacing.

The interesting thing about dealing with people's resistance is that the breakthrough in understanding often comes right at the point where it looks like all is lost. The tension often builds and builds and the other person is fighting harder and harder to prove his point when all of a sudden, some crack in the wall of resistance occurs and a small ray of light shines through. The small ray of light is followed by a very bright light, sometimes blinding. The person sees himself and/or the situation totally differently for the first time. It's nothing short of an awakening.

We coached an executive once who was an absolute tyrant. She would shake her finger at people, call them names, humiliate them in front of their peers—the list of things she did to instill fear and trembling in her people was quite long. She had a very high-level position in a Fortune 100 company and she reminded people of her power every opportunity she could.

The executive was a genius and the company very much needed her intellectual firepower so they hired us to straighten her out. In the first few sessions, the person agreed she needed to change and said she knew what she was doing. To her it was going to be as simple as doing another deal. No problem. We knew the person wasn't getting it because we continued to hear about the horrible things she was doing to her people. Not one thing had changed. In fact, it seemed like it was getting worse. The people at the very top of the organization were at their wits end and were ready to fire her when an amazing thing happened.

As a result of our intervention and the company's strong feedback to her, something finally clicked. We are not in the business of doing therapy but sometimes in the course of our work people on their own will connect back to something in their earlier lives that's related to the issues we are working on. In this case, she became aware of all the pain and suffering she had buried and how she was unconsciously acting it out on everyone around her. At the core was a good, sensitive person who was simply doing to others what had been done to her.

On the heels of this awakening, she called her immediate staff together and told them she had seen herself in a new way and was horrified at what she saw. She apologized, asked for their forgiveness, and asked them to tell her every time she got anywhere close to those old behaviors. Needless to say, her staff was shocked, elated, and greatly relieved. It was a new day in the life of the executive and her staff. You just never know with people. You may think all is lost when a breakthrough is just around the corner.

Dealing with Emotions—Theirs and Yours

All too often at work, we honor the head but not the heart. We encourage people to have thoughts and ideas but not emotions. The display of feelings in some work cultures is thought to be unprofessional—a demonstration of a lack of cool. People are expected to work like one-dimensional, intellectual beings and then we wonder why we find ourselves attending workshops and seminars on workplace violence. The unexpressed, unattended-to feelings eventually come out in some form.

Emotions are actually good things at work provided they are expressed appropriately. Emotions are energy in motion so they are essential to high performance. If you block the emotions you block the energy necessary to do the work, which is why feelings must be taken into account when you are coaching people. When people feel their feelings are being ignored or discounted, they drop out emotionally and often become the walking dead at work. Others respond by becoming raging lunatics.

Frequently, you want to ask the people you are leading, "How are you feeling?" When you do, you have to mean it. You are trying to assess where they are in the process. Do they think you are totally out to lunch? Are they angry? Are they hurt? Are they upset about something? You can't help them unless you know what's going on inside them. Sometimes we don't ask because we really don't want to hear the answer. We just want them to change. We would rather not deal with the touchy-feely stuff.

Feelings are not good or bad, right or wrong. They just are. Never tell someone she shouldn't feel a certain way or that you know how she feels. Feelings are very personal and when you tell someone she shouldn't feel this way or that you invalidate her as a person. You don't have to agree with her feelings. You just have to give the person the opportunity to express them. Encouraging people to express their feelings often helps to reduce their resistance. It clears the way for some rational, constructive dialogue about the issues.

You also have to pay attention to your own emotions. A good manager and coach has the ability to stay calm and collected on the outside when he is angry or upset on the inside. Emotionally, you want to keep one foot in and one foot out. By that, we mean you want to be emotionally engaged. You don't want to be totally void of any feelings. At the same time, you want to maintain a certain degree of detachment. If you become too emotionally or personally involved, you will most likely lose your objectivity and won't be able to help the person.

Have you ever had the experience where an employee said very hurtful things to you as a way of getting back at you for the constructive feedback you gave her? It doesn't feel good does it? Especially when you have had only positive intentions toward the person and are doing everything you can to help her. Maybe you reacted with sadness or anger. Again, your feelings aren't good or bad, right or wrong. The key is not to act them out on the person. You want to be careful not to let her bait you into a battle. Don't mirror the emotions she is expressing. You will simply add fuel to the fire. Again, stay away from descriptors such as dumb, stupid, idiot, and lazy. You won't be able to take those words back and the person will never forget it.

It's easier said than done, but your best shot is to stay calm and centered. Let the person's emotions bounce off you, at least on the outside. Remind yourself that this is about him, not you. Don't assume a defensive or offensive posture. If he is being abusive, you should firmly but politely let him know that his behavior is not acceptable and that if he cannot be civil to you, you will stop the meeting and reconvene at a time when he can behave more rationally.

Body Language Basics

When you are trying to get through to a person, you want to watch carefully for any clues she is giving you about what's going on inside her. You want to listen to and watch for the feeling content of the conversation. At the same time, you want to pay attention to what is going on inside yourself and any clues you may be giving to her.

Too often we rely solely on words when the real story is being told by our facial expressions, body language, and the tone of our voices. Have you ever had someone walk into your office and carry on a pleasant conversation with you but when he left, somehow you felt you had been done in? Have you ever felt downright strange in a conversation with a person because what she was saying didn't seem to match up with what you were feeling?

Much of the communication we receive from others and that we send to others is sent through our bodies. Most of the time it is unconscious. Our emotions are lodged in the musculature of our bodies and our bodies don't lie. Unless we purposely try to hide our emotions or communicate something different through our bodies than what we are feeling, our bodies will give us away.

When we are communicating, our emotions, of course, are more powerful than our thoughts, which means that we must pay attention to what our bodies are saying if we want to accomplish our communication objectives. For example, let's say you are coaching a person and you have a distinct dislike for the person. For some reason, you just can't seem to connect with him. If you aren't careful, your feelings about the person will be communicated through your body language. Left to it's own, your body might become stiff and closed. Your facial expressions might convey a coldness. The tapping of your fingers can convey impatience. A sigh at the wrong time could communicate disgust. Your intentions of being a positive manager might be good—you are saying all the right things—but they don't come across as positive to the person because your body language is sending the opposite message.

We have seen some amazing demonstrations of poor body language by executives. One woman had a tendency to turn her chair away from the group during meetings. When a person was speaking, she would gaze out the window. Some people thought she was sleeping. A CEO of a $14 billion company would lay his head down on the table when people were giving presentations. You can only imagine the message these two people sent with such disrespectful body language.

One of the ways we win people's trust is by being consistent in what we are feeling, saying, and doing. The more these three things are in alignment, the more people will trust you because your messages are congruent. That doesn't mean that you always say what you feel or act on your feelings. It means that you pay attention to what's going on inside you and you consciously choose your body language just like you choose your words.

For example, in the case of the employee you don't particularly like, when you are with him, listen to your body to see where the tension is. Purposely try to relax it. If you are feeling closed to the person—like you don't want to be with him—demonstrate an open body posture. Don't fold your arms in front of you or purse your lips. Let your facial muscles soften. What you communicate to people through your body is often what you get back.

▼ OUR EXPERIENCE

Winning Trust through Consistency

I coached an executive once who was extremely inconsistent in his demeanor and body language. People never quite knew which boss they were going to get—the happy, upbeat boss or the moody, aloof boss. Consequently, the people who worked with him thought him to be untrustworthy. It was so bad that every morning, the first person who had an encounter with him would observe his countenance and mood and quickly spread the word to the rest of the troops as to what they could expect that day.

When I began coaching him, he had all but destroyed his team. Interestingly, when I gave him the feedback, he was totally unaware of what he was doing. It was a revelation. In fact, he thought he was a very consistent, sensitive, nurturing manager. He had no idea what he was communicating. By being more aware and more carefully choosing his behavior, over time he was able to change their perceptions of him.

We all have good days and bad days, but the more consistent you are, the more people know what to expect, and the freer they are to concentrate on their work. We have a whole inner world of thoughts, ideas, and emotions which are communicated through our bodies in some very strange ways—ways that are not truly reflective of our intentions if we are not careful.

—Bill

As we mentioned earlier, you'll want to watch for the person's body language as well. What is it telling you? Be careful though not to over-read it. Sometimes we may think an employee is feeling one way or another when she is not. Often the best thing to do is to check it out. If you think her body language is communicating that she is angry or put off, ask her. Say something like: "I sense you are angry about what I just said. Is that true? Are you angry?"

People argue all the time that they said this or they didn't say that when the words often aren't the issue. It's what people are *feeling*—the messages they are getting from the other person's facial expressions, body language, and tone of voice. That's the arena where communication gets muddy. A glance, a shrug of the shoulders, and a sigh can all speak volumes.

Knowing When to Quit

Breaking through people's resistance can be a long, tedious process. Once you start applying these concepts consistently, our experience is that it takes a good six months to see any significant change. But how long is too long? How do you know when to give up on a person and throw in the towel? That's a tough one because no one else can answer that question for you. You don't want to give up too soon for the person's sake and for the sake of the company. Losing a person is usually expensive. And yet you can't devote time to one person at the expense of the rest of the team. Here are some questions you can ask yourself to help you determine when it's time to part company with the person or put that person in a different job.

- Is the person performing up to the job standard? If he is not, how long have I been working with the person on his issues?
- Have I done everything I can to try to reach the person?
- What are the good things the person brings to the company and what would be the cost if we lost the person?
- How easy would it be to replace the person?
- How are other people being affected by this person's behavior?
- Do I think the person is capable of making the behavior change I am requesting?
- Is there a problem or issue at play here that I may not be aware of?
- Is the person trying or is her resistance so strong that she doesn't even see the need to change?
- How much energy is this person taking from me?
- Has this person caused me to neglect the rest of the team because I am spending so much time with him?
- Have I seen any signs that her resistance is weakening?
- In my heart of hearts, do I think there is hope for this person in the job he is currently performing?

Making the hard decisions is a big part of what leadership is all about. It's also one of the most common failures of managers. You aren't doing yourself, the team, the company, or the person a favor by keeping her in a job that she isn't happy in or for which she is not suited. One person's poor performance can bring down the entire team.

Dealing with Resistance Checklist

When you are coaching a person and he resists what you are telling him, here's a checklist to help you reduce his resistance so the person can begin the work of developing new behaviors.

1. Is my feedback fair, based in fact, and relevant to the job?
   Yes ☐   No ☐

2. Have I been careful not to attack the person's self-esteem?
   Yes ☐   No ☐

3. Do I feel compassion for the person and have I demonstrated it to the person?
   Yes ☐   No ☐

4. Have I watched for signs of defensiveness and tried to determine what is behind her defenses?
   Yes ☐   No ☐

5. Do I look for opportunities to affirm the person and build his self-esteem?
   Yes ☐   No ☐

6. Do I give the person feedback at the moment I see her demonstrating the behaviors that need changing?
   Yes ☐   No ☐

7. Have I shared with the person some of my own experiences in looking at my own weaknesses?
   Yes ☐   No ☐

8. Have I been clear about the rewards and consequences for changing or not changing the behaviors in question?
   Yes ☐   No ☐

9. Have I given the person sufficient time to change?
   Yes ☐   No ☐

10. When the person resists and expresses strong emotions, am I able to stay objective and not take what he says personally?
    Yes ☐   No ☐

11. Do I watch the person's body language and ask her how she is feeling?
    Yes ☐   No ☐

12. Do I watch my own body language and try to make sure that it is consistent with the words I am speaking?
    Yes ☐   No ☐

13. Am I patient with the person and willing to live in the tension of the opposites until we can come to a mutual understanding of the issues?
    Yes ☐   No ☐

14. Do I sincerely want to see the person succeed and have I communicated it to him?
    Yes ☐   No ☐

15. If I am not able to break through the person's resistance and she is not meeting the job standard, am I willing and able to make the hard decision of terminating her and/or putting her in a different job?
    Yes ☐   No ☐

Scoring: If you answered yes to 13 or more questions, you are probably getting through to the people you are coaching. You are doing an excellent job of breaking through their resistance.

If you answered yes to 9 to 12 questions, you need to work harder at creating a sense of safety for the people you are coaching so they can own their weaknesses.

If you answered yes to fewer than 9 questions, you are probably finding yourself hitting a brick wall when you give people constructive feedback. They are probably hearing your feedback as judgment rather than information.

PERSONAL APPLICATION CORNER

Many people just give up too soon on their personal relationships. When they can't get the other person to understand them, they become frustrated and try to force the understanding which only serves to drive the person away. How many of us have thrown our hands up in despair and lashed out at a person because he just couldn't see what we wanted him to see.

When the people in our personal life resist hearing some information we wish to convey, we need to communicate smarter, not harder. We need to keep trying to find a window through which they can let in some new information about themselves and the relationship. If that's going to happen, their self-esteem must be preserved.

Something to Try: Think again of the personal relationship you have been working on. When you feel frustrated and want to attack because the person isn't hearing what you are saying, try the following:

- Take some deep breaths until you calm down.
- Listen hard to what the person is saying and play it back to her so she knows she has been heard. (You don't have to agree with what she said!)
- Stay centered and don't mirror or return the negative emotions he is expressing.
- Keep your body language open and positive.
- Discuss the issues without judging or placing blame.
- Sincerely look for a win-win.
- Present the facts as you see them. Tell the person how you feel without making her responsible for your feelings.
- Don't let the person engage you in a battle. Keep looking for the window that will allow you to understand him better and that will help him understand you.
- Resist the temptation to flee or cave in by saying something you don't mean. Stay in the tension of the opposites until you experience a breakthrough.
- Affirm the person when you can and don't threaten.
- Admit what part you may have played in the problem.
- Don't try to win.
- If you achieve a breakthrough, don't make a big deal of it—especially if the person made some concessions.

The single most important factor in saving a damaged relationship is staying focused on the mutual objective, assuming both parties want to save the relationship. When either or both parties work primarily from their own self-interests, the problem often gets worse, not better.

CHAPTER SEVEN

STEP 5
Observe and Mirror

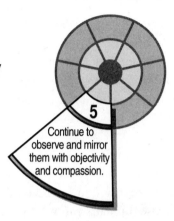

5

Continue to observe and mirror them with objectivity and compassion.

When you consistently observe people objectively and tell them what you see, you keep the lines of communication open which builds trust.

Have you ever given a person feedback, counselled her on what to do about some aspect of her behavior or performance, only to see her repeat the same old pattern? You may have thought to yourself: "What's the matter with her? Why hasn't she corrected the behavior which we both agreed needed to change?"

If only it was that easy. You tell people once what they need to do differently and presto, the change is completed. Giving feedback and creating a plan to work on a person's strengths and weaknesses is only the beginning. The real work is in applying the plan on a day-to-day basis. Old habits die hard. New skills are hard to come by. The law of inertia is a powerful force to be dealt with.

We coached a female executive who thought that once she told a person he had a problem, her work was finished. She believed it was up to the individual to deal with the problem and she expected immediate change. If she didn't see the change right away, she wrote the person up and threatened to terminate him.

Somehow she made it to a fairly high level within the company, but no one wanted to work for her and she had the highest turnover in the company. She was very naïve when it came to the subject of what it takes for people to change. She also confessed that often her perceptions of a person were so fixed that when the person did change, she didn't recognize it. Is it any small wonder that this person was passed over for two major promotions?

Change is usually a dubious process and it doesn't happen in a linear fashion. It's three steps forward, one step back. Most people have difficulty being objective about their own growth and progress. In Chapter 3, we talked about the fact that the truth is what sets people free. If they know the truth about themselves and their performance, they are in a position to do something positive about it. Your continued observations are the raw data from which you will mirror and guide people as they strive to change and grow.

People need a lot of mirroring and encouragement as they go about the arduous task of changing ingrained habits and building new skills. As we mentioned in Chapters 4 and 6, being a good mirror isn't easy because it means you have to get yourself out of the way. The more you mirror and the less you judge, the more the person will trust you and the more open she will be. The more she will seek out your feedback.

Remember, a mirror tells it like it is without any distortion. It simply reflects back what is. Just like you may not always like what you see when you look in the mirror, people may not always like what you reflect back to them, regardless of how objective you are or how well intended. If you consistently give them constructive feedback that is meaningful, the majority of people will eventually change and thank you. As a manager, it is one of the most meaningful, long-lasting gifts you can give your people. Whether they realize it or not, most people are hungry for the truth about themselves and their performance.

The Power of Attention

Your continued observation of each person accomplishes two things: 1) it provides you with the information you need to effectively coach him on an ongoing basis, and 2) it communicates to the person that you see him and that you care about him as a person, provided you are observing him with a spirit of helpfulness as opposed to watchdogging and policing.

▼OUR EXPERIENCE

Mirror, Mirror On the Wall

Once I attended a ten day women's retreat for about 30 women in the beautiful Berkshire Mountains of Massachusetts. Living in community with that many women for that long a period of time was both challenging and uplifting. One of the most memorable things about the event was how the old mirror-mirror-on-the-wall-who's-the-fairest-of-us-all game that women sometimes play with each other was changed by a series of experiential exercises.

At one of the sessions, we did an exercise that I will never forget. We were each asked to get a partner. For a period of ten minutes the partner was to give us her total, undivided attention and mirror everything she saw us do. If the person smiled, the partner smiled. If she moved her right hand in a certain direction, the partner moved her right hand in the same way. At the end of the ten minutes, the partners switched roles so that both had the experience of being mirrored.

When I was the person being mirrored, I remember how awkward it felt to have someone give that kind of focused attention to me at first. Not long into the exercise, however, I noticed how good it felt. It felt good to be seen and mirrored for exactly who I was. No judgment was involved. I was reflected back exactly as I was.

When I was the person doing the mirroring, I felt a strong human connection to the other person. I was very much aware that I was giving a gift. It felt good to be totally focused on someone other than myself. You can't look into someone's eyes for that long a period of time without seeing something of her soul. You see things about her you never saw before. You realize that behind the face is a world of experiences, hopes, dreams, hurts—a world different yet similar to your own.

I was reminded by that exercise of how little we really pay attention to one another in our fast-paced, high-tech world. Everyone seems to be rushing to complete their to-do lists for the day like there is no to-morrow. For too many of us, tasks come first and people second. We think that when we are giving someone else our undivided attention, something isn't getting done. And yet, when we do, something very profound is usually happening. A human connection is made.

Sometimes when I am stressed or when I just feel like giving someone the gift of attention, I will look the person in the eyes, block everything else out, and just focus on him—what he is really saying, his facial expressions, the music behind his words. While I am focused on him, I make a conscious effort to suspend all judgment. It's amazing how it helps me get out of myself, but more important is the response I get from the other person. He seems to get softer, more human. The quality of our interaction becomes more positive. He seems to let down his guard. Most of the time he doesn't even know what is happening, but I can see the change.

If you can learn to give your people that kind of focused attention— even if it's only for three minutes in a day—you will notice a change in how they respond to you. And you will learn a lot about them because your observations won't be fragmented.

—Diane

The Basis of Your Observation

Focus, focus, focus. It is the key to success in just about everything. When you are observing a person in her day-to-day work, the vision and developmental plan which you created with the person in Chapter 5 provides you with the framework for what to observe of her and when. You should be observing her at all times, but there are specific things you will want to watch for.

If, for example, one of the behaviors identified in the plan as needing work is that she needs to be a better listener, you will want to observe her carefully when she is in conversation with you and other people. Or let's say the plan says she needs to develop her management skills, you will want to watch for things like how well she communicates expectations to her people, how well she delegates tasks, whether or not she gives her people feedback on a regular basis—all of the things that go with being a good manager.

The goals you outlined in the developmental plan are your binoculars. They will help you bring into focus the things that are critical to the person's success. If you observe some annoying behaviors that aren't part of the plan, either adjust the plan if the behaviors are critical to the person's success or let it go. Your job is to stay focused on the competencies and behaviors that have been identified in the plan as being critical to the person's success. Don't let the person's little idiosynchrasies or your own baggage get in the way of what's important. Don't sweat the small stuff.

What to Look for

When you observe your people you want to watch for two things:

1. Information that will help you understand the person better, and
2. Demonstrations of the person's behavior which you can use to help him understand himself better.

It always astounds us when we come across a top executive, which we do frequently, who thinks he has great insight into people and who has people all figured out. He thinks he knows just what people are capable of, how they will react, and what they will say. Such arrogance hurts everyone.

Never assume you have a person figured out. If you think you know most of what you need to know about a person, your observations will be distorted. You will see with judgmental eyes. Situations and people are constantly changing—especially if they are growing—so you will want to observe her almost with the eyes of someone who doesn't know her at all. Sometimes what we already know about a person can hinder our getting to know her better. The better you understand a person, the more equipped you will be to bring out the best in her and support her in achieving the objectives of the job.

Once we were doing a training program for a group of people on how to be assertive in the workplace without being labeled a maverick. There was one shy woman in the audience who barely spoke during the program. She was a woman in her early 50s, a little out of shape. At the beginning of the program, she shared with the group that she was terrified of speaking up in a group so she was never able to get her ideas across. Consequently, her career had suffered.

At the break, she came up to us and pulled something out of her wallet. Proudly she showed us a card with her picture on it. It was her Harley-Davidson Club membership card. She proceeded to tell us that when she and her husband divorced when she was in her late 40s, she bought herself a big Harley-Davidson and learned to ride it. She rides regularly with a club and has toured a good part of the country.

Never in our wildest dreams would we have expected that from this woman. Having this piece of information about her helped us work with her in the workshop so that she could transfer the strength and confidence she feels on her bike to the workplace. That's what makes working with people so interesting. You just never know what is behind the face or picture they are putting out to the world. The key is to get behind the picture so you can understand them better.

In addition to trying to understand your people better, you will want to observe them closely so you can give them real-world, real-time examples of their behavior—examples that are relevant to the goals you have established in the plan. Let's say you have a person working with you who gets very short with other people when he is under pressure. Very often people are oblivious to the messages they send to other people. They don't even know when and how they irritate others. If you see a person get short with another person, observe all the details of the behavior and interaction so you can play it back to him exactly as you saw it. When a person gets enough examples reflected back to him surrounding a specific goal, he starts to make the connection. He begins to understand himself better. Self-awareness is the first step in the change process.

Sometimes we can see another person more clearly than she can see herself. The key is to get her to see herself from the perspective of others. People often feel misunderstood and unfairly judged when they get negative feedback because their intentions are different from what people are perceiving. When they feel they aren't being seen for who they think they are on the inside, they usually feel hurt. Most of us want very much to be understood and liked.

In order to get people focused on how others are perceiving them, we must speak to them in specifics. In order to do that, we first have to learn the art of observing in specifics. Exactly what did the person do that was off-putting? What did his voice sound like? What did his body language look like? Judging from the body language and response by the other person, what was the impact of his behavior? Take him back to the scene. Have him relive the scene and describe his experience in the situation in detail.

What you are looking for are coachable moments. A coachable moment is any situation that offers you an on-the-job opportunity to teach the person something relevant to her developmental goals. If you aren't watching, you can easily miss them. That's why it is so important to stay focused on the goals. We will talk more about how to get the most benefit out of coachable moments in Chapter 8.

Feedback from Others

As the person goes about the implementation of his developmental plan, the feedback you receive from others will be crucial. What you see with your own eyes is not enough. Feedback from others is essential to finding out if and how the person is progressing. What you see is not always what other people are getting.

We coached an executive once who had great insight into his problem but he didn't have a clue as to how to fix it. He was a very task-oriented person who would attack jobs with a vengeance. When he got immersed in work, nothing else mattered much but the work. He was actually a very warm, sensitive person and those who worked very closely with him understood him and appreciated his many fine qualities. The people who didn't work with him on a day-to-day basis saw him very differently. They saw him as cold, indifferent, and arrogant.

He knew he was coming across as insensitive but when he flipped into work mode he became totally unaware of the specific things he was doing to create such a perception. Because he didn't know, it was imperative that we go to the people who perceived him negatively and ask them for feedback as he worked to increase his awareness and improve his behavior.

When you seek feedback from the people who work with the person you should be careful not to undermine him in any way. The tone of your voice, the words that you choose, the timing—everything should convey your desire to help the person. Ideally, people should be giving the feedback directly to the person as well as to you. The more you can create an environment where people request and give constructive feedback as a way of helping each other eliminate their blind spots and grow, the better.

Considering the Context

Have you ever had the experience where someone suddenly observed you doing or saying something and you knew that you were going to be misunderstood? The other person would have to know the larger context in order to understand why you were doing what you were doing. It's as though you were caught doing something that you did not do. Or have you ever accused someone of something only to find out that you jumped to conclusions and misjudged the person?

As you observe your people, you always want to look at them in the context of the situation and what is going on around them. Here are some questions to help you make sure your observations are complete.

- What might have prompted the person to say or do what he did?
- What do I know about the culture of the organization which might have motivated the person to behave in such a way?
- What are the events surrounding the situation or behavior in question?
- What other facts about the situation do I need in order to understand the meaning behind the person's behavior?
- Have I spoken with the necessary people in order to get the true picture?

Here's where your clear screen is important. If you are looking for information to confirm the judgments you have already made about the person, you probably won't be able to get a true picture. In fact, you probably won't even be motivated to look at the bigger picture because your mind is already made up.

Finding Time

All of this may seem very time consuming, but once you learn to apply these concepts, you can do it automatically in the course of your day. Giving feedback should be a way of life—not an event. It's mostly a matter of paying attention and increasing your awareness of what is going on around you. You can pick up information simply by walking into a person's office or from a simple exchange with a person. The secret is to look at people with new eyes: eyes that are always open, eyes that can see beneath the surface of things, eyes that know when to look for more when they think they may not have the whole picture, eyes that see the person as well as her performance.

Updating the Plan

In Chapter 6, we talked about the importance of creating a plan that is flexible and easily updated. The more you observe a person, the more clarity you will have about his strengths and weaknesses. As work situations, goals, and people change, the priorities should also change. If you aren't constantly observing the person, the work, and the work environment, the person's developmental plan will probably be soon outdated. Your focus will not be as razor sharp as it should be. Or you may still be focused, but you will be focusing on things that are not critical to the success of the person, the job, and the organization at the present time.

Many people have a resistance to planning because they feel the plan will restrict them. Some feel that it is a setup for failure because everything is changing so rapidly. The facts they used in their planning can change overnight, which can render the plan obsolete. They fear they will nonetheless be held accountable for reaching the objectives in the plan.

If your observations and fact gathering point to the need to change the person's developmental priorities, by all means, change them. In fact, if you aren't constantly changing the plan, it probably means the person isn't continuing to grow. The plan should change with the person. Your action steps should actually change frequently.

The more you observe a person, the more you will see which of your coaching techniques are working and which aren't. You will want to constantly add new things for people to try. This will keep the learning fun and interesting. Much of the work you will do in helping people change old patterns of behavior is experimental. What works with one person won't work with another. The key is constant observation.

Ongoing Observation and Mirroring Checklist

We've said it many times in this book already, but it bears repeating: To be a good manager and coach you must be able to get yourself out of the way. You must have a clear screen. For that reason you will want to develop the habit of checking in with yourself periodically, particularly when you are observing a person. Here are some questions to help you make sure you are observing a person in such a way that you are able to mirror the person effectively.

1. Do I make a conscious effort to observe the person on a regular basis?
   Yes ☐   No ☐

2. Do I give the person frequent, undistorted mirroring?
   Yes ☐   No ☐

3. When I observe the person, do I give her the benefit of the doubt?
   Yes ☐   No ☐

4. When I observe the person, do I look for positive change in him?
   Yes ☐   No ☐

5. As I observe the person and ask others about their perceptions, do I do it in a spirit of helpfulness and in a way that preserves the person's integrity?
   Yes ☐   No ☐

6. Am I careful to stay focused on the priorities outlined in the plan?
   Yes ☐   No ☐

7. Do I constantly look for coachable moments?
   Yes ☐   No ☐

8. As I gain new information about the person, do I allow my perceptions of her to change?
   Yes ☐   No ☐

9. Do I take into consideration the situation and context when I am observing a person's behavior and performance?
   Yes ☐   No ☐

10. Do I use the observations and feedback I receive from others about the person to adjust the plan accordingly?
    Yes ☐   No ☐

Scoring: If you answered yes to 8 or more questions, you are doing an excellent job of observing and mirroring your people on an ongoing basis.

If you answered yes to 5 to 8 questions, you need to pay more attention to your people if you are going to coach them effectively.

If you answered yes to fewer than 5 questions, you have little basis for coaching your people effectively.

PERSONAL ACTION CORNER

Observing and mirroring people in our personal relationships can be very tricky. The minute our mirroring borders on judgment and criticism, the other person usually becomes defensive and closed to what we are saying. The dictionary says a mirror is something that faithfully reflects or gives a true picture of something else. That means you reflect the positive as well as the negative.

Something to Try: Think about the relationship you have been working on. How often do you mirror back to the person what you see? Do you pay enough attention to the person to even be able to mirror him? For the next week, try doing the following:

- Observe the person very carefully. Try to look past some of her annoying behaviors (if she has them) to see who she truly is. Make a mental list of what you think her strengths and weaknesses are.
- Whenever you can (without overdoing it), reflect back to him some positive aspect of his personality. It might go something like this: "You know I was watching you this morning getting the kids ready for school. You are so organized and efficient. I appreciate the way you help to keep our home working." The point is, let him know you notice his positive qualities.
- If there is something the person is doing that really annoys you, find the right time and place to reflect back the part of her that she may not see. (This is often harder to do with spouses than with children.) You might say something like: "When we were at dinner tonight with the Joneses, you interrupted me when I was speaking and you changed the subject. You probably weren't aware that you did that (give her the benefit of the doubt), but when you interrupt me I feel discounted."

Whether it's a spouse, child, or employee, when you mirror a person with love and compassion, you help to heal him. You celebrate him as a person and allow him to be human. What a different world this would be if we all got a little more of that!

▼**OUR EXPERIENCE**

The Challenge of Being a Good Mirror

Sometimes the hardest feedback to hear is that delivered by our families, particularly our children. After all, we are supposed to be their teachers, aren't we? We are supposed to have the answers, or are we?

One day my 35-year-old son decided to give me some feedback about how I was living my life—particularly my choice of friends. My how things change with age. My son relayed to me that he thought my friends by now should be of a different ilk. According to him, they should be doctors, lawyers, artists—people who were more professorial, people of status, people he could respect. Point blank, I was hanging around with the wrong kind of people. He wondered what I was getting from my relationships.

My first reaction was to smack him and give him a piece of my mind. I was hurt and angry that he would judge me in such a way. If we are honest, most of us will probably admit to wanting to appear flawless, at least in the eyes of our children. Perhaps that's why parenting our children before the age of five can be such a joy because at that age we are perfect to them.

When you think about it though, wouldn't it be boring and nonproductive to our personal growth if all we ever heard were positive things about ourselves? Most of us in our heart of hearts actually yearn for someone to tell us the real truth, and then still love us. While I wanted to lash back at my son, my better self listened, thanked him for his candor, and encouraged him to continue to tell me the truth as he saw it.

At the same time, I did defend myself by saying that I like my friends because they are real to me. They are not afraid to show their weaknesses and vulnerabilities. They do not hide behind roles and they do not pretend to have it all together. There is no pretense when we are together which frees me to be myself. He looked at me quizzically and seemed to absorb what I was saying. It took just about everything in me not to give back to him some negative mirroring. In the end, I think we both had a better understanding of one another.

—Bill

CHAPTER EIGHT

STEP 6

Teach and Guide

When you teach people, you let them know they are worth investing time in which helps to win their trust.

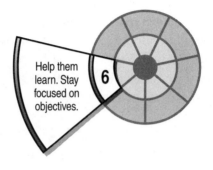

Help them learn. Stay focused on objectives.

6

If you look throughout history at famous leaders, the majority of them were teachers. In fact, true leaders are almost always in teaching mode. That's how they get people to follow them—by inspiring, informing, and helping people be more than they thought they could be. As managers, our job is the same: to bring out the greatness in others.

In Chapter 7, we talked about the importance of constantly observing your people and mirroring back to them what you see—similar to what a good sports coach does. But it can't stop with the mirroring. Once they have seen and acknowledged the part of their performance that needs improvement and/or the skills they need to acquire, you have to provide learning experiences which will enable them to change and grow.

Motivating People to Learn

One of the problems with many adults is that when they reach a certain age, learning is no longer a priority. People learn from experience, which is sometimes a very costly, painful teacher, but they don't necessarily seek out formal learning opportunities. Your job as a manager is to get them back in the active learning mode. Your challenge is to get them excited and committed to their own growth and development to the point where they are constantly on the lookout for new learning opportunities. Your job is also to facilitate their learning, not to spoon feed them every step of the way. The goal is to resurrect in the person the curiosity of a three year old.

You want to encourage each person to get in the habit of reviewing his developmental plan almost daily. He should look at the priorities outlined in the plan and then look at his daily calendar to determine what opportunities for learning might present themselves. Opportunities for learning could include any of the following:

- A meeting or situation in which the person can practice the application of the skill(s) she is working on (e.g., conflict resolution, listening, sales)
- Observing a person who is an expert in a particular field or who regularly exhibits a strong skill in a particular area
- Seeking out people, internally and externally, who are subject or skill experts and asking them questions
- A situation where he feels he is being stretched and challenged
- Classes, books, tapes that specifically address the developmental priorities outlined in her plan
- Asking for on-the spot feedback from others

In each learning situation, you want to encourage the person to do the following:

- Listen, observe, and/or practice, depending on the learning situation
- Extract the key learning from the experience
- Practice the learning
- Reflect on what the person did well and how he can improve
- Apply and practice the new learning and repeat the steps above

Learning that results in significant behavior change is rarely a one-time experience. Learn, practice, reflect. Learn, practice, reflect. That's how people grow. The practice is essential. The repetition of a particular behavior over and over is what breaks the old patterns and/or builds new skills. Reflection is also essential because that's when the ah-has occur—the in-depth learning. Without the person's reflection and your validation of her reflection, a person can practice but she may be practicing the wrong things. As one person said, practice doesn't make perfect—perfect practice makes perfect.

How to Know If Learning Has Occurred

You will know that real learning has taken place when the person is able to transfer his insights and knowledge to different situations. For example, let's say you are working with a person who is extremely quiet and introspective. You have been encouraging the person to be more assertive at weekly staff meetings. You've given him some techniques to help him feel comfortable interjecting his thoughts into the conversation. Some time later, you observe him in conversation with someone outside the department who has a tendency to dominate the conversation. You observe him successfully engaging in a two-way dialogue in which he makes sure his views are heard.

The greatest behavior changes occur when people are able to continuously apply and build on the things they are learning and when they are able to make the connections between what they have learned and applied in one situation and how it applies to another situation. Each time they do, they reinforce what they have learned. Learning becomes a continuous process. If they aren't able to transfer their learning to different situations they have probably learned by rote or mimicking. Anyone can repeat a behavior in the exact same set of circumstances. In other words, did they get the words and the music or did they just get the words. This is where your observations and mirroring are so important. Sometimes people think they've got it but they haven't.

It's a good idea to encourage each person to keep an ah-ha or learning journal. Whenever she has a flash of insight and understanding, ask her to write it down as soon as she can. It's helpful if she can also describe the situation in which the insight occurred. When she feels she has mastered a new skill or a new task, ask her to write it down. Committing it to writing helps to reinforce the learning. The learning journal can also be a motivator for the person. Looking back in her journal over time can help her see how far she has come.

Developing Skills

Every organization's success rests heavily upon having people with the right competencies and skills. All too often we throw good people into jobs and expect them to acquire the skills they need through the hard teacher called experience. Experience and practice are essential to mastering a skill but not until people have some formal instruction. Otherwise experience can be a very costly teacher.

Depending on the type of skill, the formal instruction may take the form of a class, seminar, on-the-job instruction, role playing, case study, discussion, simulation, or hands-on practice. Let's say you are teaching a person a technical skill. Figure 8.1 shows a step-by-step process for ensuring the success of your coaching session.

With some modification, this four-step process can be used for teaching less technical skills as well. You will still want to prepare the person for the learning, present the material, allow for practice, put her on her own, and follow up.

Let's say, for, example, you are teaching someone how to confront situations more effectively and resolve conflict. After you put him at ease and prepare him for the instruction, you will give him the basic principles involved in resolving conflict. You can practice applying the principles by doing some role playing with him. You can encourage him to practice the skills in his work relationships and bring his experiences back to you for reflection and discussion.

FIGURE 8.1 Four-Step Training Process

> ### I. Prepare the Person
>
> - Put the learner at ease. Don't put undue pressure on him by rushing through the training. Express your confidence in him but don't make it sound like you expect him to master the learning in no time.
> - Explain the purpose or objectives of the skill or task to be learned. Give the reasons why it's important that the person learn what you are teaching her.
> - Find out what he already knows about the subject. He may already have some knowledge or experience which you will want to build upon.
>
> *(continued)*

FIGURE 8.1 Four-Step Training Process *(continued)*

- Stimulate some personal interest or motivation for learning the skill. People learn best when they want to learn. Tell the person the benefit she will receive.
- Create an environment conducive to learning. The physical environment should be comfortable and well equipped. It should be quiet so the person can focus.

II. Present the Material or Task

- Break the task or skill into basic elements, steps, or phases. People learn best when a task is presented in manageable chunks.
- Present one step at a time using clear, simple language. Never use vocabulary that is unfamiliar to the person.
- Give the person no more than he can absorb at one time. Everyone learns at a different pace. Don't rush through it.
- Stress key points or critical ideas. Share with the person any tricks of the trade that will enhance her understanding and help her remember.
- Demonstrate the skill or task while you explain. When you can, demonstrate and instruct at the same time. The more senses you engage, the better.

III. Practice—Let the Person Try

- Have the person perform the task. Don't ask him to do so until you are fairly sure he will have a success experience.
- Correct mistakes and errors as they occur. Don't wait until the person is finished before you tell her what she did wrong.
- Have the learner repeat the task, explaining each of the steps as he goes. By having him explain what he is doing while he is doing it, you reinforce the learning.
- Check to make sure the person understands why she is doing things in a certain way. Make sure she isn't performing by rote.
- Have the person continue to practice until you are sure he has mastered it.

IV. Follow Up—Check Results

- Put the person on her own and tell her where she can go for help. This will help the person remain calm, knowing that if she forgets, she has someplace to go to ask questions.
- Check frequently on his performance. When you do, don't appear as though you are policing him. Do so in a spirit of helpfulness.
- Check and review her understanding of the task. Repeat instruction if necessary.
- Taper off to normal supervision once you are assured he has achieved mastery.

Watching for the Coachable Moments

Coachable moments are those golden opportunities to teach people on the spot. Your coaching moves from theory to practicality quickly when you observe them on the job and provide them with immediate feedback. And it doesn't have to take a lot of time.

We once worked with a company that was as committed to coaching as any organization we had ever seen and its bottom line reflected it. The company was a large national retail chain with hundreds of stores all over the country. Talk about focus and attention. Every day in every store, every manager was required to do at least one two-minute coaching drill with every salesperson in the store. Coaching was not a nice-to-do activity, it was a must do. It was as important as ordering inventory, stocking the shelves, and maintaining the store.

The two-minute coaching drill usually went something like this.

- The manager observed the salesperson in a customer sales situation.
- After the customer left, the manager took the person aside and asked her how she thought she did.
- The manager then gave feedback to the person as to how she could have done better.
- The manager and salesperson role-played the real-life sales situation that had just occurred using the manager's suggestions and the employee's self-reflection.

The two-minute coaching drills were used for a whole host of purposes, including improving performance in all kinds of areas, encouraging cross selling and add-ons to purchases, correcting mistakes, and maximizing sales. Here's a list of some of the specific ways the managers used the two-minute coaching drill.

- Used slow times for coaching practice. If, for example, salespeople weren't recommending enough product, they would take them in the back room and review the basics of what they called Score 4 (sell four products in every sale) and the Big 3 Questions (ask the three questions which lead to sales).
- Taught salespeople how to transition from selling one product to selling another.

- Showed how to make confident recommendations without sounding pushy.
- Helped salespeople think through items to suggest.
- Instructed salespeople how to handle customer turn downs.
- Showed salespeople how to ask open-ended questions.
- Trained salespeople how to listen and focus on customer needs.

Managers used every coaching opportunity as a chance to teach a principle, practice it, and then get commitment for continued performance. Some managers would actually do role plays with salespeople as they unpacked shipments. Some quizzed salespeople on products during down times. Managers were constantly in coaching mode.

Role playing was such a way of life that often a manager would do a role play with a salesperson and soon after, the role play they had just completed became a reality on the sales floor. Coaching was so entrenched in their culture that managers coached the managers below them and salespeople even coached managers! As managers constantly coached salespeople, the salespeople were so programmed to deal with customers in specific ways that when managers didn't follow the instruction they had been giving, the salespeople let them know.

To reinforce the power of coaching even further, managers were asked to submit their best coaching stories which were periodically published in a book and distributed throughout the entire company. Anytime anyone in the organization had room for improvement—not just salespeople—coaching was the tool managers used most to help the person achieve peak performance.

Once you start looking for them, you'll find that coachable moments happen all the time. Before you seize the moment, you will want to ask yourself these questions.

- Is the time and place appropriate?
- Is the person in a frame of mind to hear what I am saying?
- Am I prepared to coach the person and offer my undivided attention?

Here's a dialogue between a supervisor and a receptionist named Pat. The supervisor is passing through the reception area as Pat is greeting a guest. The supervisor overhears the conversation between Pat and the guest and recognizes it as a coachable moment. After the guest is escorted to his meeting, the supervisor has this conversation.

Supervisor: Pat, I was just passing through and saw what transpired between you and the guest. How about if we take a time out and talk about it.

Pat: Okay.

Supervisor: We have talked about the fact that you are the first person people meet when they walk into the company, so the way you treat them is very important. First impressions are lasting. How do you think you did?

Pat: Honestly, I wasn't paying much attention because I was busy tracking down a Federal Express package on the telephone. I can only do one thing at a time.

Supervisor: I know you sometimes have a lot to juggle, but it is so important that you greet every guest who walks in the door with a smile and pleasant greeting. If they have a coat, show them where the coat closet is. Politely ask them who they are here to see. From what I saw, you seemed a bit annoyed with the guest because he was interrupting you from what you were doing. I'm sure it wasn't intentional but that's how it came across.

Pat: Yeah, well I was frazzled. What do I do when the phone is ringing and two people have given me things to do, like track down a package, and a guest walks in the door?

Supervisor: Well, remember your first responsibility is to greet and announce guests and help them feel welcome. If you are on a telephone call, unless it is urgent, ask the caller if she can hold while you greet the guest. Think of it like you are greeting someone who is visiting your home. You would want that person to feel welcome and comfortable. You have a very important job, Pat. How people are treated when they first walk in the door tells them a lot about the company.

Pat: Okay.

Supervisor: There's no one in the lobby now. I'm going to walk through the door. I want you to greet me like you think guests should be greeted.

From here, the supervisor would role play with the receptionist, point out what she did well, and offer suggestions for improvement if necessary. In this situation, we see that the supervisor coached the person while the experience was fresh in the mind of the supervisor and the receptionist. The supervisor didn't just criticize the receptionist. The supervisor took the opportunity to reinforce with the person how important she and her job are to the company. The supervisor spoke about specific behaviors that were expected, role played with the receptionist, and then gave feedback again. Hopefully, the next time the supervisor walks through the reception area she will see different behavior.

Sticking with It

Getting people to commit to their development plan is like getting people to commit to an exercise program. It takes the same amount of dedication, will power, and discipline. One reason people work with a personal trainer when they are exercising is to have someone hold them accountable. Here are some of the things you can do to ensure that learning and growth actually happen.

- Set aside a specific time every week or every two weeks to meet with the person, even if it is just for 15 minutes or a half hour. At this meeting you will want to refer back to the developmental priorities outlined in the plan and ask the person what he has done in implementing the action steps. Ask him to tell you about any experiences he may have had relative to the priorities and action steps.
- Look for as many opportunities in as many different situations as you can think of where the person can apply the action steps in the plan. Encourage her to be on the lookout for such opportunities as well.
- Keep the routine aspects of the person's development from becoming too mundane and boring. Remind him that real winners are people who consistently do things they don't want to do. Help him to see the heroics of committing to something and slugging it out everyday—just like athletes or musicians who do daily drills, even on days when they don't feel like it.
- Refer back frequently to the vision you established in the developmental plan. Remind the person why she is taking the action

steps—what rewards/benefits await her upon the accomplishment of her developmental goals.

- Help the person push through periods when he has plateaued by giving him extra praise and encouragement.

Not only does the person have to stick with it, so do you. If she has agreed to try something or apply one of the action steps in a situation that you both know is coming up, make sure you follow up. Unless you hold people accountable for what they agree to do in the developmental plan, they can easily slip back into old habits and behaviors.

Breaking Old Habits

One insightful executive we had been coaching for quite some time described his experience this way: "I know I still have a lot of the same tendencies and weaknesses, but the difference today is that I understand myself better and I can better anticipate when one of them is about to rear its ugly head. Now I can choose a different behavior and consequently achieve a different result than I got before—and that feels very good."

Many of people's ingrained patterns of behavior are deeply rooted. As we tell people, "There is no cure—just improvement." Self-awareness is the first step. Once people know they have a certain tendency, you want to help them identify the times and situations when they are likely to demonstrate the behavior(s) they wish to change. Help them recognize the internal signals and external signals when they are approaching or are already in a behavior. The sooner they can catch themselves, the better.

One executive we coached frequently got very agitated when people didn't respond or perform in meetings the way he wanted them too. He became sarcastic and condescending which didn't do much for his image as a leader. By asking him to reflect on why he got so upset and what was going on inside himself when those occasions arose, he learned to temper his behavior. When he started feeling tense in his body, when he started to hear a certain tone in his voice, he learned to calm himself, manage his body language, and respond differently. Some of the same emotions still arose within him in those situations, but he learned to not act them out.

Other people can also provide a person with cues that they are in a negative behavior. A person, for example, who talks too much might want to watch for the impatient look or the glazed-over look that people get when they are tuning out of a conversation. You can also encourage the person to actively enlist the help of other people. Depending on the behavior and the person's vulnerability in a situation, she can ask designated individuals to tell her when she is in a particular behavior. The more good mirrors a person has, the better.

Once people begin to understand themselves and see the need for changing some aspect of their behavior, it becomes somewhat of a game for them—a game to see how quickly they can catch themselves and alter their behavior. With a little encouragement, people will come up with their own techniques for observing themselves and changing their behaviors, which is why together you should be constantly updating the developmental plan. Every time the person and/or you come up with something new to try, write it in the plan. The more creative, the better.

Managing Failures

One of the most impressive executives we ever worked with was a man who didn't believe there was such a thing as failure. It was not part of his vocabulary. At the young age of 37, he was one of the top leaders in his company. He was adamant about the fact that every lost sale, every mistake, was an opportunity to learn.

Today, at the age of 46 he is the CEO of a major corporation. One of his mantras to this day is, "How you fail in one situation provides the learning that will help you win in the next situation." One of the foundations of his success lies in being able to turn what some people call failure into an eventual success.

One of your jobs as manager is to get people comfortable with risk taking and that means getting them comfortable with some failures. Every failure should be looked at as a learning experience. If people can learn from their mistakes, it is no longer a failure.

The more people risk, the more likely they are to have some falls. Many work environments are fairly risk adverse so this can be a difficult one for people. We've said that your relationship with the person is the foundation for the change which is why trust is so essential. If people don't believe they have a safe environment with you, they won't risk looking weak or inadequate.

Here are some of the things you can do to encourage people to take risks and look at failures as steps to learning and growing.

- Express your belief in the person and your support, especially when he lapses or falls down.
- Frame the person's experience for her. Remind her how difficult change is and that it doesn't happen overnight. Especially for the conscientious overachievers, help them with their perfectionism.
- Remind the person that this is different from completing a project. There is no end. It is not black and white, right or wrong. Learning is a lifelong experience. In the early stages, especially, you will want to position the person's experiences as creative experiments—trying on new and different behaviors until she finds the ones that work.
- Frequently remind the person of his successes. Affirm him as a person—not just his accomplishments.
- Make sure you have given the person the right amount of challenge—not so difficult that she fails, but not so easy that there is little motivation or feeling of success. As she masters certain tasks and behaviors, keep adjusting the priorities in the plan so she has appropriate challenges.

Checklist for Teaching and Guiding

The toughest part of managing is finding the time to give people the training and guidance they need. The more skill you acquire in mirroring them, the less laborious it will feel and the greater results you will achieve. Here's a checklist for being a good teacher.

1. Do you keep people focused on the priorities and action steps in their developmental plans and hold them accountable?
   Yes ☐   No ☐

2. Do you constantly seek out opportunities for people to practice their skills and new behaviors and do you encourage them to do the same?
   Yes ☐   No ☐

3. Do you encourage people to self-reflect and discuss their ah-has and experiences with you?
Yes ☐   No ☐

4. Do you help people to constantly build on what they are learning and are you constantly updating their developmental plans accordingly?
Yes ☐   No ☐

5. Do you make sure people have had proper instruction before you encourage them to apply new skills?
Yes ☐   No ☐

6. Do you constantly watch for coachable moments?
Yes ☐   No ☐

7. Do you discipline yourself to stick with each person through the difficult phases of change and do you encourage each person to do the same?
Yes ☐   No ☐

8. Do you help people anticipate the times and situations when they are most likely to display the behaviors they wish to change? Do you help them recognize the external and internal signals?
Yes ☐   No ☐

9. Do you give people the right amount of challenge—not too easy and not too difficult?
Yes ☐   No ☐

10. Do you help people pick themselves up and dust themselves off when they fail?
Yes ☐   No ☐

Scoring: If you answered yes to 8 or more questions, you are doing an excellent job of helping your people learn new behaviors and skills.

If you answered yes to 5 to 8 questions, you need to work harder at being a good teacher in your role as manager.

If you answered yes to fewer than 5 questions, you are probably providing your people with few opportunities for growth and development.

PERSONAL ACTION CORNER

When we teach another person something we know, whether it is through our example or through formal instruction, we share ourselves with him. The wisest teachers, of course, are those who are both teacher *and* student. They never share their knowledge to feel superior—only to help others. They believe they can learn something from everyone. Their willingness to learn from others and share what they know enables them to form meaningful connections with other people.

Just as every manager must be a teacher, so must every parent. Teaching a child something you know—whether it is tennis, car mechanics, or cooking—is a wonderful way to spend time with her. It's a way to bridge the generation gap. Sometimes the most meaningful, unplanned conversations about life occur when the parent and child are focused together on something other than the issue. It can be a time for the child and parent to relax together, to express things they might find hard expressing otherwise. This can be true, not just with children, but with other people in our lives as well.

Something to Try: Ask one of your children or someone else in your life if he would like you to teach him something (pick something you think he would enjoy learning). When you teach him, do the following:

- Make sure you set a relaxed tone for the training session. Do not put him under any pressure.
- Make the learning fun. Do not set up any expectations.
- Teach him at his pace and ask him frequently if he understands.
- Give him plenty of encouragement, even if he is struggling with the new learning.
- Give him adequate demonstration and instruction before you let him practice.
- Compliment him when the instruction is over and set up a follow-up time for when you will continue (only if he wants to).
- Go get an ice cream or something together so the two of you can talk about your experience or just to continue the good feeling of having shared some time together.

CHAPTER NINE

STEP 7

Recognize, Celebrate, and Reinforce

Look for improvements and opportunities to celebrate.

7

When you recognize and celebrate a person's success, it tells her you see her as more than a means to getting the job done. It says you value her as a person, which builds trust.

The need to be validated and recognized is a fundamental human need and when it goes unmet, the needs of the job often go unmet. If you have been around small children you are well aware of their constant requests for validation and recognition: Look at me. Watch me dance. Watch me hit the ball. Look at my pretty picture. Adults are not that different. The only difference is that when we grow up, we pretend we don't need it. We act as though we can get by without it. There is an unspoken rule in most organizations that says the higher up in the organization you go and the more we pay you, the less feedback, praise, and recognition you should get. Almost every executive we have ever coached complains of this fact.

When you are coaching people, your recognition of their efforts and successes is what fuels their willingness and desire to keep trying. People who are very inner-directed and self-motivated will keep trying even if they don't get your recognition, but even with them, it is still a boost when they receive recognition. And don't expect people to tell you when they need some recognition and encouragement. Most people in the world are starved for just a little recognition and affirmation from someone.

Sincerity Is Key

Have you ever had the kind of boss who periodically slapped you on the back and told you, "Good job" as though he was checking something off his to-do list for the day? If the recognition is to have any effect, it must be heartfelt and genuine, otherwise people will experience it as manipulation. So how do you convey sincerity? One way is to cite in specifics the positive things you have observed. When you do, it tells the person that you are paying attention to her—that you appreciate what it has taken for her to accomplish what she has accomplished. For most people, that is worth every bit as much as a pay raise. Beware, however, of praising every small thing a person does or saying the same thing over and over—good job, good job. Overpraise and praise that is spoken in clichés loses some of its meaning.

Don't Praise and Hit

Sometimes managers praise people first as a way of preparing them for the bad news that follows. Sometimes it is appropriate in a formal coaching session to sandwich criticism between praise but there should be plenty of times when you just praise them. If you constantly praise people and then deliver the *but,* they will feel that their efforts are never quite good enough. They won't even hear the praise because they know the bad news is coming.

Managers are sometimes afraid to deliver praise by itself for fear the person will stop trying or get the impression that he doesn't need to improve anymore. If you have that attitude, people will feel that their change process is a hopeless battle—that they will never get there. People need to be recognized for their efforts as well as their results. That doesn't mean you praise them for their hard work when they don't reach their performance objectives (provided it is due to some failing on their part). But it does mean you praise them for their efforts in developing new skills and changing behaviors. They may still have a long way to go in mastering the skill and/or changing their behaviors, but they should still be recognized for the progress they have made. Certainly you want to focus on the gaps—how far they have to go—but sometimes you simply want to focus on how far they have come.

Most people have a fair amount of self-doubt which is the enemy of personal growth and development. Your recognition of their progress is sometimes the only thing that will keep them from giving up and abandoning ship. For some people, it may well be the first time in their lives that they have had an authority figure encourage and cheer them on. Appearances can be very deceiving. Sometimes it's the people who appear to need it least who need it most.

Celebrate the Moment

The recognition you give a person should take a variety of forms. There's nothing like sharing the sweetness of success in the moment. The success may not even be noticeable to others, but when you see, for example, a behavior that a person has worked hard to change, don't wait to acknowledge and celebrate it. Do it right then and there. Your recognition in the moment may be nothing more than a thumbs up or a wink of the eye—anything that let's the person know you have witnessed her victory. You can talk about it later in a more formal coaching session, but don't miss the moment. Those shared moments are what create a bond between you and the person. People carry those small demonstrations of affirmation with them in their minds for a long time.

Watch What You Praise

We had a client once who praised everything people did. Consequently, the praise and recognition lost some of its meaning and significance as we mentioned earlier. Go back to the priorities and action steps in the developmental plan. Make sure you place particular emphasis on praising demonstrations of the desired behaviors identified in the plan.

To a large degree, people change and grow as a result of rewards and consequences. Every time you reward a specific behavior, you reinforce it and increase the likelihood that the person will do it again. If you overpraise something that is not that important, people will work very hard at that which is unimportant just to get your praise. That doesn't mean you shouldn't praise an accomplishment or behavior that isn't in the plan—just make sure you place the proper emphasis.

Make It Personal

A good rule of thumb is to criticize the behavior when you need to but praise the person. People need to know they are more than tools for getting the job done. It's trite but true: everyone wants to feel special. As we said earlier, when you recognize them, make sure you cite the specifics of their successes or accomplishments. The vehicle you use for communicating recognition is also important. An e-mail or a small flower and a handwritten note—gestures that show you put some thought into it and took some time—speak volumes to people. Sometimes you may even want to ask someone else in the organization, usually at a higher level, to recognize the person in some way.

▼**OUR OWN EXPERIENCE**

Treasured Acknowledgments

The other day I was going through some of my files when I found an old tattered yellow memo dated August 15, 1973. It was a congratulatory note from my boss on my first major accomplishment in my first real job right after college. As I read it, I instantly recalled the sheer thrill I felt when I first read it some 27 years ago. It was as though someone had given me this invaluable gift—a gift which helped my confidence immensely. The fact that I still have it speaks to how much it meant to me.

Years later, I had a boss and mentor who was a master at recognition. He found all kinds of ways to let people know how much he appreciated excellent work. I remember on one occasion when the accounting department was working into the wee hours of the morning on a big project, he, the CEO, was there running the copy machine for them— letting them know he appreciated their sacrifice.

Perhaps the most impactful thing he did in the way of recognition was to handwrite on his personal stationary (fine stationary at that) a letter to each of his direct reports telling them what he appreciated about them in the past year. Most people barely have time to breathe during the busy holiday season, but the letters came each year without fail. Those letters, too, were treasured by all.

As we were writing this chapter, Bill shared with me something he did one year when he was CEO of Drake Beam Morin. In addition to writing each of his direct reports a letter, he bought them a child's gift.

For some he bought a doll, for others it was an electric train or a doll house—everyone got something different.

To his surprise, people responded to those gifts with greater excitement and appreciation than any gift he had ever given at work. It was as if the child in Bill was speaking to the child in them. The gifts were special because they were things the people would have never bought for themselves. They were gifts that, for a time at least, whisked them out of the responsibility-laden world of the adult and brought them back to the wonderful feelings of childhood. Gifts that said the giver cared about them in a personal way.

—Diane

We think money is the big motivator and it certainly is when people aren't being paid enough or when they don't have enough to provide for their basic needs. Once that happens though, money doesn't go that far unless it is some huge sum of money. Even if the large monetary rewards are there, people still need personal recognition from you. Money feeds the pocketbook. Some of these other more personal forms of recognition feed the soul.

Don't Make Promises You Can't Keep

When you are creating the vision of the person's success in the developmental planning, make sure you don't promise him a reward that you may not be able to deliver. If you even imply that if he does this or that you will promote him, in his mind it is done. That may be your intent, but today's business world is changing too rapidly to be able to promise almost anything in the way of promotion or pay. Nothing can erode trust more than failing to deliver on a promise.

You also want to stimulate in people a desire to grow and develop for reasons other than pay and promotion. One person we coached was extremely upset because he had been meeting his objectives and hadn't been promoted as he thought he should have. His boss hadn't promoted him because of some of his interpersonal skills and because he was too driven and aggressive. Getting him to want to improve and grow for no other reason than the mere satisfaction of doing so was essential.

We asked him to think about what he truly valued. By changing the focus from his extreme need to be promoted (which he did not need for financial reasons) to simply working on himself, he eventually got what he had stopped driving so hard for—the promotion. By that time, after months of arduous work on himself, the promotion was secondary. He seemed to be more proud and pleased with the personal progress he had made than with the promotion.

Balancing Recognition

Remember, every time you recognize and/or affirm one of your people publicly, which you should do from time to time, you are sending a message about what you value. People will also extract their own meanings out of your public recognition of people. Whenever you recognize a person on your staff you can be sure that most of the other people on your staff will be thinking thoughts such as: Is my manager playing favorites or does the person really deserve the recognition she is giving her? Have I received equal recognition for accomplishments that are of equal importance and significance? When was the last time my manager recognized me in such a way? Naturally, you are going to like some of your people better than others, but it should be your secret. People should feel they are treated equally—not necessarily the same, but equal.

Getting Comfortable Giving Praise

Some people have difficulty giving praise and recognition. It just doesn't come natural. Sometimes people have difficulty receiving praise which can create some awkwardness on the part of the giver and the receiver. If you are one of those who withholds recognition for whatever reason, just remember how much most people need and appreciate it. Find ways of recognizing people that are comfortable for you. Never assume that people know how you feel. Sometimes people will act like they could care less what you think of them but that is usually just a defense. Even if they have difficulty receiving it, don't stop giving it.

Recognition Checklist

How and when you recognize people has an enormous impact on their personal growth and development—for some more than others.

Here's a checklist to make sure you are recognizing and rewarding people effectively:

1. Is the recognition you give people sincere and heartfelt?
   Yes ☐   No ☐

2. Do you frequently give people stand alone praise—praise which is not followed by a criticism?
   Yes ☐   No ☐

3. Do you look for small improvements that you can celebrate with people?
   Yes ☐   No ☐

4. Is your praise and recognition personal? Do you cite in specifics the positive things you have observed about them?
   Yes ☐   No ☐

5. Do you make sure the form of recognition you give people is appropriate for the achievement?
   Yes ☐   No ☐

6. Do you recognize the person as well as his accomplishment?
   Yes ☐   No ☐

7. Do you consider how the recognition you give one person will be perceived by other people who work for you?
   Yes ☐   No ☐

8. Do you look for creative ways to recognize and celebrate people?
   Yes ☐   No ☐

9. Do you pay particular attention to recognize those successes and behaviors that are critical to the persons and the team's success?
   Yes ☐   No ☐

10. Are you careful to not make promises you can't keep?
    Yes ☐   No ☐

Scoring: If you answered yes to 8 or more questions, you are doing an excellent job of recognizing your people in a way that promotes the behaviors you are seeking.

If you answered yes to 5 to 8 questions, your people may still be in need of meaningful recognition from you.

If you answered yes to fewer than 5 questions, your people are probably demotivated due to lack of recognition.

PERSONAL ACTION CORNER

Sometimes the smallest words of encouragement and/or affirmation can make an enormous difference to people. The right praise and recognition given at just the right time have been even known to change the entire course of people's lives. All of us, of course, enjoy the recognition of the world but nowhere do we need it more than in our homes, in our personal relationships. We need to know that our loved ones appreciate us for who we are.

Something to Try: For one week, look for opportunities to acknowledge and recognize the person in the relationship you've been working on. Don't praise her for every little thing she does but try to affirm her in some way every day. At least once during the week, think of some thoughtful way—some way beyond words—to express to her what you appreciate about her. If she has been working on something—maybe she has been trying to lose weight or stop smoking or maybe she is going to school at night to get a college degree—look for a way to affirm and encourage her.

CHAPTER TEN

Coaching Challenging Personalities

Have you ever managed a person to whom you just couldn't get through? No matter what you said or did, the relationship never seemed to work and any attempts at coaching either made things worse or had little effect. Welcome to the world of management. Just when you think you've figured out how to manage people effectively, a situation presents itself that leaves you scratching your head in bewilderment.

We've given a lot of guidelines for coaching people in this book but there is no one formula for managing people, just as there is no one formula for raising children. That's what makes it so challenging. Each person is unique and different. Each has his own baggage, his own personality, his own style of communicating, his own views of authority figures—all of which can be possible sources of conflict between you and him. As managers, our job is to treat all people fairly but not the same. People need customized managing and coaching—particularly those who are challenging to work with.

In the introduction to this book, we said that the most effective managers have a basic understanding of human behavior. In this chapter, we will give some insight into people who present particular challenges and some suggestions for how to work with them. Of course, the better you understand yourself, the better you can understand the dynamics that may be going on between you and a difficult employee. Sometimes we need to adjust and change. Knowing when we are the problem and when the employee is the problem is sometimes difficult to discern. Our own egos, of course, will always point the finger at the other person. Here are some challenging personalities and suggestions for working with them.

The Passive-Aggressive Person

The passive-aggressive person is a tough one to deal with because you are never quite sure how she really feels. Her aggression is cloaked in passivity which sometimes makes it difficult to recognize. So what are some examples of passive-aggressive behavior? It can manifest itself in a multitude of ways, such as:

- Withholding important information as a way of disempowering another person
- Being pleasant and nice to a person and talking viciously about them to others
- Setting themselves up to be the victims in situations when in fact they are the perpetrators
- Playing subtle mind games that keep people on their guard
- Refusing to deal with conflict directly
- Punishing another person by shutting down and refusing to communicate
- Doing something hurtful to another person and then pretending not to know what the person is talking about
- Making another person feel guilty as a way of getting the person to do something

Passive-aggressive people are usually highly manipulative. They can be extremely creative and devious in the ways they get people to do what they want them to do. If you don't know what you are dealing with, it can feel like real crazy-making. Your gut tells you something is wrong but on the surface everything is fine. Here are some general rules for dealing with passive-aggressives.

- Don't play the same game with them. It will only make matters worse.

- Try to understand their motives and keep them in the forefront of your mind when you are dealing with them.
- Stay centered. Do not let them push your buttons. (At least don't let them know they are pushing your buttons.)
- Don't reward the behavior in any way.
- Be direct with them.
- Depending on the situation, point out their contradictory behaviors.

Here is an example of how you might deal with a passive-aggressive employee who you know has real issues with you and is talking behind your back, but refuses to engage in any meaningful dialogue with you about the problem. The manager is in the middle of a coaching session with the person when the manager addresses the issue of his passive-aggressive behavior.

Manager: Jack, we have been talking about a lot of issues and throughout our entire conversation you have not been engaging with me. I get the sense that you are upset with me for some reason but I don't know what it is.

Jack: No, I'm not upset with you. Everything is fine.

Manager: Well, I want to tell you what it looks like from my position. Your body language is very closed. Whenever I bring up sensitive issues and try to get some conversation going about them, you shut me out. What is that about?

Jack: I don't know what you are talking about. Nothing is wrong. As far as my body language goes, it happens to be very cold in here.

Manager: Jack, I have heard from other people inside the department and outside that you have been saying less than complimentary things about how I am managing this department. You obviously have a right to your feelings, but it doesn't do you, me, or the team any good when you criticize what goes on here to people who can't do anything about it.

Jack: Is this a threat? Are you telling me I shouldn't express my views to my coworkers?

Manager: No. You are putting words in my mouth. I did not say that. What I am saying is that I want to help if there is a problem, but I can't address it if I don't know what it is. Why are you afraid to talk to me about what's bothering you? I am open to hearing what you have to say. I can take criticism, but I have difficulty dealing with problems that come to me through the grapevine. Help me out here.

We see in this conversation that the manager said what he was thinking, seeing, and feeling but he did it without threatening Jack. He simply stated it as fact. He brings the behavior out in the open but doesn't attack him for it. Instead, he poses some logical questions that will hopefully cause Jack to think twice about what he is doing. He also makes it safe for Jack to talk about his issues. If Jack continues to deny that there are any problems, the manager should remind Jack that the problems will remain his until he is willing to discuss them with him.

The Angry, Belligerent Person

The angry, belligerent person is similar to the passive-aggressive person in that they are both angry. They just express it differently. A person with these characteristics can be very dangerous to a work group because she infects people with her negativity. Sometimes these people are so vocal and forceful that they silence the majority who don't share the same views. They are so loud it *appears* that everyone feels the same way. Here are some of the characteristics of the angry, belligerent person.

- Sarcastic
- Highly critical
- Short fuse
- Impatient with others
- Knows it all
- Insensitive to the feelings of others

People who are often angry and belligerent at work are usually angry about something other than work. Their anger is misplaced. The likelihood is that they are angry about something in their past or current personal life and are venting that anger at work. They rant and rave about this and that but it is usually just a smoke screen. They may not even realize that's what they are doing which makes them even more dangerous. They have little or no self-awareness and understanding. Here are some guidelines for dealing with them.

- Don't return their anger with anger. Stay centered.
- Mirror what you think, see, and feel.
- Ask them why they are so angry.
- Help them see that the intensity of their reactions is not appropriate to the event. (Be careful on this one. Don't tell them they shouldn't feel a certain way).
- Set strong boundaries with them. Do not let them be abusive.
- Help them realize they are not helping themselves by staying angry all the time.
- Encourage them to get help if you think it is needed.

In the example that follows, the manager is trying to deal with an employee who is always losing her temper and saying inappropriate things to the manager and some of her coworkers. Again, the manager has already set the stage for the conversation, so we are entering in the middle of a coaching session.

Manager: Carla, let's talk for a few minutes about your anger.

Carla: My anger? What—I'm not supposed to have any feelings? Sure I get angry because this is such an inefficient organization and management doesn't give a flip about the employees. Yes I am angry. I have every right to be and I am not the only one. This place makes me sick to my stomach.

Manager: Carla, do you see what just happened? I made a statement and you just took off. Your face got red, your voice got loud. I simply said, "Let's talk about your anger," and you blew up at me.

Carla: Sure, I blew up at you. You are just like the rest of management. You want everyone to be pleasant, make nice, and get the work done. You don't care that the employees just got screwed in our new contract. If management cared one iota about us, they would never have even proposed the terms of the recent contract. What are we to think, huh? You take this and that away. You make these crazy demands.

We have no rights here. All management cares about is making a buck. We are fed up!

Manager: Carla, you are making a lot of accusations and speaking in these broad generalities. I can't address any of your concerns because you are so angry. Your anger is getting in the way of our having any kind of meaningful conversation.

Carla: Oh, who cares! We are just prisoners of management. The best thing to do is just wait it out until we retire.

Manager: Unless you can calm down and speak civilly to me, we will have to discontinue this conversation. Can you collect yourself enough so we can at least have a conversation about what is bothering you?

Carla: Okay.

Manager: Carla, I want to hear about your work concerns, but I am concerned about the fact that you are angry so frequently. Do you enjoy being angry so much of the time?

Carla: No, but I can't help it when all this stuff is going on around me.

Manager: Has your anger been a problem for you in other situations and relationships in the past?

Carla: No. I just have strong feelings about things.

Manager: So, it has never been a problem for you?

Carla: No, not really.

Manager: What do you mean, "not really"?

Carla: Everybody gets mad sometimes.

Manager: But Carla, do you see that you are angry almost all the time? I want to help you with your anger but I think you need to take some responsibility for how you express your emotions at work. I want to see some improvement in this area.

Carla: Oh, yeah. Wait till my union rep hears about this.

Manager: Carla, I'm trying to help you. Don't you see? This is what I would like you to try the next time you find yourself getting really angry . . .

From here, the manager discusses with Carla ways that she can control her anger at work. The manager may suggest that she read a few books on the subject, take a class, maybe even call the employee assistance program. As the conversation concludes, the manager is very firm and direct about the behavior change that is expected even if Carla disagrees that she has a problem.

In this example, the manager mirrored back to Carla what she was seeing and didn't let Carla bully and sidetrack her by getting off the subject of her anger. The manager did not return Carla's anger, but let her know what was expected of her. The manager did not allow Carla to talk disrespectfully to her or put her on the defensive. She came from a position of helping rather than judging and demanding.

The Social Gossip

Social gossips often spend more time feeding the grapevine than working. They seem to have a hotline to what's going on in the company. Sometimes their information is amazingly on target and at other times, it is filled with rumors and innuendos. In any event, the social gossip wastes a lot of his own time as well as that of others. Sometimes his gossip can be very hurtful to others. Here are some of the characteristics of the gossip.

- Extremely social
- Often hangs out in other people's offices
- Frequently on the telephone
- Has huge networks

People who are social gossips are getting something from their behavior. There is a payback. It often has to do with a person's need to feel important and in-the-know. It gives them a feeling of power and control. Social gossips do a lot of implied bartering: "I'll be your friend if you tell me this information and vice versa." When people share gossip, they often share a false sense of connectedness with one another. They bond for the moment over the juicy piece of information they have about someone else. This is a tough behavior to confront because it is almost always done in secrecy. Here are some suggestions for dealing with social gossips.

- If you see them on the telephone a lot and/or spending a lot of time in other people's offices or cubicles, ask them if they are bored and need more work.
- Keep them so busy and challenged that they have little time for gossip.
- If you are passing through their work area and you feel they are gossiping, find some reason to interrupt them. Subtly let them know that you know what they are doing.
- If you know for a fact that they have either told confidential information to others or spread hurtful rumors, confront them directly.

Here's how a manager might deal with a person reporting to her who is constantly spreading office gossip.

Manager: Alan, I would like to talk with you about something that is a sensitive issue. I know you have a lot of friends in the company—not just in this department but in other departments as well. I think that's a good thing. I'm concerned, however, about the amount of time I observe you on the telephone on what appears to be non–work-related calls. When you are not on the telephone, I often see you hanging out for long periods of time in other people's offices.

Alan: But wait a minute. Don't I always get my work done on time? My last performance review was near perfect. What does it matter if I am getting my work done? Besides, I thought this company was a big believer in teamwork.

Manager: You do get your work done on time which brings me to the next point. If you have that much time to spend with others talking about things that aren't work related, maybe you aren't challenged enough at work. Also, you may be getting your work done but keeping others from accomplishing what they need to get done.

Alan: This is starting to feel like kindergarten. Do you keep track of every phone call I make and every time I stop by for a friendly chat with a coworker? Besides, how do you know we aren't talking about work?

Manager: I am not keeping track. It is so obvious that I can't help but notice. Your body language, the tone of your voice, a number of things lead me to believe that you aren't talking about work much of the time. Besides, I have been told by some of my peers in other departments that they frequently see you in their areas, whispering to their staff members. Just yesterday, I was passing by your cubicle and I happened to overhear you talking about an affair that someone in another department is having. I can't control what you talk to other people about but I feel I need to tell you that I don't like it when you engage in company gossip. From what I see and what others tell me, that is what you are doing. Maybe you aren't, but that's what it looks like to me.

Alan: Well, if that's what you believe, I guess there's nothing I can do to change your mind.

Manager: Yes there is. I'd like you to focus more on your work. In fact, I have a special project coming up that I think you would be perfect for—one that I think you would enjoy.

The manager then describes the project. As she concludes the conversation, she asks Alan how he is feeling as a way of finding out where he is with the feedback. She concludes by restating her expectations.

Again, the manager tells Alan how things look to her but is careful not to make any accusations which she cannot substantiate. She responds to his attacks in a matter-of-fact fashion by clarifying what she said and what she didn't say. She does not return anger with anger. Instead of trying to force Alan to admit that he is guilty, she focuses on something positive—an interesting project which will hopefully keep him busy so he doesn't have as much time to gossip.

The Overly Sensitive, Conscientious Person

The overly sensitive, conscientious person is sometimes difficult to coach because her extreme sensitivity keeps her from hearing what you are trying to say. She often reads into things that simply aren't there. Here are some of the characteristics of the overly sensitive, conscientious person.

- Very thin skinned
- A high need for approval
- Very critical of herself and sometimes others
- Can be very defensive and emotional
- Focused on pleasing others

The overly sensitive, conscientious person tends to be a perfectionist. Her need for perfection usually stems from some insecurity. From her perspective, she is either a supreme success or a total failure—there is no in between. Here are some guidelines for dealing with this type of person.

- Give them plenty of recognition and praise.
- When giving them constructive criticism, tell them what you are *not* saying. In other words, frame the criticism with plenty of positives.
- If they get defensive, ask them why they feel the need to do so.
- Don't withhold constructive criticism from them because of their sensitivity.
- If they cry or get emotional at the slightest criticism, encourage them to look at that tendency.

Here's a vignette from a sample coaching session between a manager and an overly sensitive employee.

Manager: Mary, I'd like to talk to you about the amount of time you are spending on the weekly reports that you do for our internal customers. I see you laboring over them and taking a long time to complete them. I think you need to look at how you are spending your time. They shouldn't take that long to complete.

Mary: I work very hard. I don't waste time. Don't I always get my work done on time? I take work home every night so that I can stay on schedule.

Manager: I know you get your work done on time. That's not the point, Mary. I know you are a very hard, conscientious worker. Sometimes I can't give you other work, though, because I know you are pouring over those reports. We need to find a way to work a little faster and more efficiently. Some of the information you include in those reports is not necessary and I see how you are so careful to dot every *i* and cross every *t*.

Mary: But I think it's important to do things right. You don't want me to make errors, do you? Now I'm really concerned. I thought you were really pleased with my work and now I hear you telling me that I'm not getting enough done and that I need to be more efficient. I pride myself in being one of the top performers in this department.

Manager: Mary, I'm not saying you aren't an excellent performer. You do very good work. I'm just trying to help you free up some time so you can take on some other responsibilities.

Mary: Well, give me the extra work. I can handle it.

Manager: I know you can get it done but eventually you are going to burn yourself out if you keep trying so hard to make everything absolutely perfect. This is not a criticism. I'm just trying to help you be more effective.

Mary: Are you upset with me about something else? You seem to have been a little distant with me lately.

Manager: No, Mary. What makes you think I am upset about something else? I've been very busy lately so I may not have had as much contact with you as usual, but it has nothing to do with you.

Mary: Oh.

Manager: I think you are sometimes overly sensitive, Mary. Have you noticed that almost every time I give you the slightest suggestion for improving your work you get very defensive and read things into what I am saying? I'm glad you care about your work, but sometimes I think you take things too seriously. You are doing fine but you are not perfect and I don't expect you to be.

The manager then discusses with Mary specifically how she can spend less time on the internal customer reports. In this situation, the manager uses one example to address a broader issue. The issue is not the time she is taking to do the reports, it's her whole approach to her work. The manager keeps working with Mary on how she is perceiving what she is saying. She is straight with Mary about her concern but reassures her that she is a valuable employee.

▼**OUR EXPERIENCE**

Zero Tolerance for Criticism

I had an administrative assistant once who prior to coming to work with me had never received a performance review. She was a perfectionist who was accustomed to getting plenty of verbal praise, but had been deprived of the opportunity to grow and develop.

Periodically, I would have coaching sessions with her to give her feed-back and to discuss how we might work better together. Ninety-five percent or more of the feedback I gave her was excellent but there were some areas where I thought she could improve. What a shock I was in for.

When I gave her the constructive criticism, which I thought I gave in a very positive fashion, she hit the ceiling. She was incensed. No one in her entire career (she was in her 40s) had ever given her one ounce of criticism, so she thought I was being picky and totally out of line. Nothing I could say about how wonderful I thought her work was and how valuable she was made any difference. She quit over a few con-structive comments. Some people can't take any criticism, but that should not deter us from speaking the truth, even if there are unfor-tunate consequences.

—Diane

Checklist for Coaching Challenging Personalities

These are just a few of the coaching challenges you may face. No doubt you can add to the list. While each person must be treated fairly but differently, there are some general guidelines you can keep in mind when you are working with a person that presents a challenge.

1. Do I tell the person what I see, think, and feel in an objective, non-judgmental fashion?
   Yes ☐   No ☐

2. Do I try to understand what is behind the problematic behavior or personality trait?
   Yes ☐   No ☐

3. Am I careful not to reward the negative behavior or personality trait?
   Yes ☐   No ☐

4. Do I set good boundaries for myself and let the person know when his behavior is inappropriate?
   Yes ☐   No ☐

5. Do I stay centered and refrain from giving back to the person the negative energy she sends to me?
Yes ☐   No ☐

6. Do I let the person have his feelings even when I don't agree with his perceptions?
Yes ☐   No ☐

7. Am I careful not to let myself be manipulated by the person's emotions?
Yes ☐   No ☐

8. Do I maintain the proper balance between firmness and compassion?
Yes ☐   No ☐

9. Do I use examples of the person's behavior to help her see her patterns?
Yes ☐   No ☐

10. Do I end the session by restating my expectations, even if the person doesn't agree with the feedback I have given him?
Yes ☐   No ☐

Scoring: If you answered yes to 8 to 10 questions, you are doing a very good job of dealing with challenging personalities.

If you answered yes to 5 to 8 questions, you need work on understanding and dealing with challenging people.

If you answered yes to fewer than 5 questions, the challenging people who work for you are probably driving you crazy!

PERSONAL ACTION CORNER

One of the common parenting pitfalls is comparing one child to another. We label one child the model child and another the problem child. The more we label, the more we reinforce the behaviors we like and/or dislike. All too often we get what we expect.

Sometimes a challenging child is just different. Who knows why one or more children from the same family can have virtually the same upbringing and turn out totally different? The key is to try to understand the challenging child and work with her to overcome whatever weaknesses or problems she may have.

Something to Try: Think about one of your children who is challenging to you. If you don't have children, think about a challenging person in your life. You may have a dynamic going on with the person that is extremely uncomfortable for both of you. No doubt it keeps repeating itself. If so, ask yourself these questions.

- What is it that the challenging child or person needs from me?
- What is it about him that drives me crazy? Why does he push my buttons?
- Do I feel manipulated by her? If so, what can I do to set boundaries for myself?
- How can I mirror him without judging him?
- What can I do to keep myself from reacting in ways that are counterproductive to the person and our relationship?
- What can I do to rebuild some bridges of trust which may have been broken in the past?

CHAPTER ELEVEN

External Coaching for Managers

If you have a manager reporting to you whom you have coached effectively and you are unable to get through to her, then this chapter is for you. Or maybe you have a manager loaded with potential whom you want to move along faster, but you don't have the time to spend with him. You may need the help of a professional outside coach. Or maybe you are a human resource professional and you know there is a problem with one or more of the company's middle- to higher-level managers— a problem which is not being dealt with by the person's manager. You will also find this chapter helpful.

The Higher People Go, the Less Coaching They Seem to Get

Most of the middle- to high-level managers we work with report that they get little or no feedback on how well they are performing. You can be sure the people they report to and the people who report to them have some very definite ideas about how they are performing, but none of that information is shared with the executives. They are left to read the subtext and focus on the only thing that appears to matter to those above and that is the bottom line. And we wonder why more than half of all change initiatives fail.

The answer to the question of why so few executives receive feedback perhaps can be found in the myth that when you rise to a certain position in an organization you no longer need feedback from others—you have arrived. Or maybe it's because the people executives report to aren't comfortable giving feedback either. It's easier for most executives to focus on the business results than it is to focus on the harder issues of personal performance.

In a perfect world, everyone in an organization would be getting feedback and not just from their bosses. People would mirror back their managers' behaviors, managers would mirror each other, and people at all levels would constantly get the information they need about themselves in order to accomplish the objectives of the job so they can each grow as a person. Creating a coaching culture within an organization requires real commitment from the people at the top. But the return in terms of productivity, quality, growth, and competitive advantage can be enormous.

Managers need coaching every bit as much as the people below—if not more. Think of the responsibility that rests on their shoulders. When executives have blind spots or when they are lacking in particular skills or they are having difficulty getting up to speed fast enough in new jobs, the cost to the organization and the people is huge. If the manager's manager doesn't have the courage or expertise to give the person honest feedback, an executive coach is often the answer.

What Is Executive Coaching?

Executive coaching is a hands-on, one-on-one process between an executive and an external coach. There are internal executive coaches and mentors, but in this case we are referring to professional coaches hired from the outside for the express purpose of working with mid- to high-level executives. The executive coaching process is designed to help the executive learn faster and more effectively and produce greater results for the organization. Executive coaching is one of the best ways to maximize the talents of people in key management positions. By helping executives reflect on how they are getting their results, executives are empowered to make better decisions and be better leaders.

When to Use an External Coach

One could present the case that if managers throughout the organization were doing the job of coaching, there would be no need to hire external coaches. To some degree that is true. Working with executives, however, often presents a different set of challenges which make it difficult for someone inside to do the coaching. Here are some reasons for hiring an external coach.

- There may not be many people in the organization with the time and/or expertise necessary to work with the executive.
- Executives at higher levels are often reluctant to be vulnerable to people inside the organization. An external coach provides a safe, nonthreatening way to examine and work on skills and behaviors.
- Power and politics are removed from the situation because the coach is an objective outsider with no agenda other than to help the person and the organization.

Who Needs an Executive Coach?

Coaching has come a long way from the time when it was used primarily to shape up people who were not doing the job. Coaching is still used to help people who are underperforming, but more and more it is being used for developmental purposes. In either case, after an executive works with a coach for a while, the person invariably recognizes it as a gift, almost a luxury. The person realizes how much faster she can learn through one-on-one relationships with experts and she realizes how helpful it is to have a safe place for processing what is happening within her and around her. It's like having your own personal mentor.

There are different types of executive coaching, depending upon the developmental needs of the executive. Here are some of the common uses of executive coaching.

- *Skill development.* An executive may need some work on one or more of the competencies required for the job. The executive, for example, may be performing quite well but needs work on presentation skills.

- *Performance.* The executive is having difficulty meeting the performance standards for the job. In this situation, the coaching would be very focused on the specific goals and objectives of the job and how to achieve them.
- *Developmental.* The executive may be an excellent performer who the company wants to move ahead faster. These are generally high-potential people who are meeting the requirements of the current job but who may not be quite ready for the next position. Sometimes it is worthwhile to invest the money in hiring an outside coach for lower- to mid-level managers if they have a lot of potential.
- *Remedial.* Coaching is a last-ditch effort to save a person. External coaches are often hired to simply delay the inevitable. All too often, the external coach is brought in too late. Too much damage has already been done. No one, including the person, believes there is much hope.
- *Executive's agenda.* Sometimes executives have their own personal reasons for hiring a coach such as the person described in the example below.

▼OUR EXPERIENCE

Career Crises Resolution

Once an executive of a well-known company asked if I would serve as his executive coach. He said he had some issues he wanted to process with me. I quickly learned that he had been the creative genius behind a highly successful product which had become a major part of our culture. Having been with the organization for almost 20 years, he was feeling restless and unfulfilled. Much of his heart and soul had gone into his work in the past, so the decision of whether to stay or leave was a difficult one to say the least.

In the process of doing the 360-degree interviews, one of the recurring themes was that the executive was a creative genius, but he was weak in his management skills which caused difficulty for him and others. When I interviewed his boss, the CEO, I asked if he had given the person feedback about his management skills and if there had been any consequences for not performing that part of his responsibility up to standard. The CEO replied: "No. I haven't given him much feedback and there have been no consequences because frankly, I don't want to have to compete with him on the street. He is too valuable to lose, so I have not wanted to upset him."

When I gave the person feedback, I told him I thought he had been spoiled. Because he had this great gift he did not have to do some of the other things that others were expected to do. He had been deprived of the opportunity to grow and develop because people throughout the organization were afraid to give him feedback and hold him accountable.

After working with him for a while, he finally came to the conclusion that it was time for him to develop a different relationship with the company. He felt he would not be able to address those areas of his development which needed work while in his current position, so he converted the remainder of his contract to a consulting role. While he is greatly loved and admired by people at the company, everyone, himself included says that it has worked out for the best.

This is a perfect example of how companies lose when they don't give executives feedback. It's also an example of how executive coaching, even when it is initiated by the executive himself, can create a win-win for the person and the organization.

—Diane

New Leader Coaching

Almost every newly hired executive could benefit dramatically by working with an external coach in the first six to eight months of the job. Research studies show that more than 40 percent of newly hired senior executives fail in the first 18 months of the job. They fail for a number of reasons, the most common of which are they are unclear about what is expected of them, they are unable to adapt fast enough to the new culture, and they are unable to build a sense of team among peers and those they are leading.

One large company we were consulting decided it wanted to improve its marketing capabilities. It wanted to be more proactive, more aggressive in marketing its products and services. It decided to hire the best professionals from the best consumer product companies in the country, so it paid over $3 million in search fees to hire five marketing executives from companies such as the Pepsi Cola Company.

Within one-and-a-half years all five executives left the company. In their exit interviews, they all cited the same reasons for leaving. They did not feel supported, appreciated, or respected. They found the environment stifling and couldn't understand why the company would spend the money to hire them when the company didn't want to listen to them and utilize their expertise. It was a very expensive lesson. The human resource department estimated that the company had spent $7 to 8 million to learn that it did not know how to assimilate people into its culture.

In today's business environment, a newly hired executive must be able to hit the ground running. She must be able to produce solid results quickly. A good coach can help a newly hired executive ensure that the honeymoon period doesn't turn into a nightmare. The coach can help facilitate the development of the relationship between the executive and her boss. The coach can get feedback on the executive's performance early on before opinions of the executive become too solidified. Most important, the coach can anticipate any potential problems and help the executive adapt to the culture.

Participants in the Coaching Relationship

In order for coaching to produce solid results for the individual and the organization, the following people should be involved in the process:

- *Coachee.* The executive who is receiving the coaching may or may not be the person who initiates the request for a coach but he must be open to the process. The more committed the person is to the process, the more he will get out of it and so will the company.
- *Coach.* The coach is the director and coordinator of the coaching process. In addition to orchestrating the assessment and 360-degree interviews and doing the coaching, the coach should keep all of the concerned parties in the communication loop. The coach is the team leader.
- *Coachee's boss(es).* The coachee's boss is critical to the entire process. She should work with the coachee and the coach in setting the coaching goals and objectives. The boss should also participate in the 360-degree interviews. Periodically, the boss and the coach should meet so they can give each other feedback on the progress they see the coachee making. The boss should mirror and reinforce the behaviors the coach and coachee are working on, which is why it is important that the coach and boss stay in close contact.

- *Human resource executive(s).* Human resource executives are the internal managers of the process. They are often the ones who will find and hire the right coach for an executive. There may be more than one human resource representative involved, depending on how the function is organized. For example, in a large organization, the line human resource manager would be involved as well as the human resource representative responsible for executive development and/or organizational development. Before the coaching begins there should be some kind of written agreement which spells out what will happen in the coaching process and who will do what over what period of time.

Confidentiality Is Key

One of the things that makes external coaching different and effective is that the executive is free to express things that he might not feel comfortable expressing to people within the organization. In any coaching relationship, trust is the key, which means confidentiality must be maintained. Sometimes a coach walks a fine line in this regard. The coach must keep everyone in the loop but must never divulge personal/private information the coachee would not want her to divulge, unless, of course, it is information that reveals a legal liability to the organization or suggests danger to the coachee and/or others.

While the company is paying for the coach's services, the coach's first loyalty must be to the coachee. There should not be a conflict here because what is best for the coachee is almost always best for the company. In any event, the coach and all of the people involved in the process must discuss and agree upon the confidentiality boundaries. The coach works for the interests of all parties. The coach is brought in by the company, however, it should be a win-win for everyone.

Selecting the Right Coach

In the previous chapters, we have been talking about the manager as coach. In this chapter, of course, we are talking about hiring an outside coach for mid- to high-level managers or executives.

Coaching has become somewhat trendy today, so a lot of people are hanging out their shingles. Executive coaching is a substantial investment of time and resources so you will want to be very careful in your selection.

You may choose an independent coach who works solo, or you can select a coach through a coaching company which offers a variety of coaches with different backgrounds and expertise. Whomever you hire, the coachee should have some say in who is selected. The coachee should be given two or three coaches to choose from after human resources has ensured their qualifications. In most cases, the coachee should be discouraged from working with an external coach with whom he or she has a personal relationship.

Checklist for Hiring the Right Coach

Hiring the right coach for an executive is essential. If an executive has never had a coach before and the relationship doesn't work, it could sour the executive on the entire process. Here are some questions you will want to ask to determine if a person is the right coach for an executive.

1. Does this coach have adequate experience in working with executives on this level?
   Yes ☐   No ☐

2. Does this coach appear to have the ability to develop a strong, trusting relationship with the executive?
   Yes ☐   No ☐

3. Does the person have a style that is compatible with the executive's style?
   Yes ☐   No ☐

4. Does this coach have the skills and business background required to meet the coaching objectives?
   Yes ☐   No ☐

5. Is the coach someone the executive can respect?
   Yes ☐   No ☐

6. Does the coach appear to be a team player and can he be flexible?
Yes ☐   No ☐

7. Does the coach appear to fit with the culture of the organization?
Yes ☐   No ☐

8. Is the coach a person of integrity and does she appear to be one who can deliver the truth to the organization and the executive?
Yes ☐   No ☐

9. Does this person appear to be one who has great insight into people and situations?
Yes ☐   No ☐

10. Does the coach have an executive presence?
Yes ☐   No ☐

The coaching results will only be as good as the match between the coach and the executive. Finding a coach who has the expertise and who has a connection with the executive is not always easy. It's best to take your time until everyone is comfortable with the prospective coach.

PERSONAL ACTION CORNER

Have you ever had a relationship that you cared about deeply but for some reason you just couldn't seem to get it to work? Sometimes it's because we don't have the necessary interpersonal skills or there is so much old baggage that we stay mired in the past. Sometimes things change which affect the entire dynamic of a relationship. Whatever the reason, relationships can be very complex and hard to understand. Our best intentions and hard work sometimes are just not enough. We need an outside coach of some kind if the relationship is to survive and flourish.

Something to Try: If you have been applying the technique we have suggested at the end of each chapter to one of your personal relationships and the relationship is still not working, you may want to enlist the services of a counsellor. Here's what a good counsellor can do for you.

- Help you and the person better understand the true nature of the problem.
- Help both of you take greater responsibility for your part in the problem.
- Teach you communication skills for dealing on your own with day-to-day problems which may arise between the two of you.
- Help you set healthy boundaries that support the relationship.

Going to a counsellor is not a sign of failure in a relationship, as some may think. It's actually a sign of strength. We aren't born with interpersonal and communication skills and in our culture we don't see a lot of healthy modeling of such skills. Problems are inevitable in every relationship. The question is, what are you doing about them?

CHAPTER TWELVE

Coaching High-Performance Teams

Many of the top executives we coach report that they have a problem getting their people to work together as a team. What they usually have is a leadership problem. Once we coached a CFO of a major company, for example, who was the consummate micromanager. He had his hands into everything and consequently had control of very little. He was chastised by his superiors for the way he was operating his function and was told he must create a greater sense of team among his people.

After we worked with the CFO for almost a year, he developed a totally new skill set—that of leading teams. Instead of focusing all of his efforts on the work, he spent his time developing an environment and work process which encouraged the people in his group to work together. He became the facilitator of his team rather than a policeman of the work and it made all the difference in his own effectiveness and the effectiveness of the people reporting to him.

The most successful companies today are those that create organizations where people act like they own the place, where they are passionate about what they do, and where they are encouraged to challenge management. What we have just described are the primary characteristics of a team-based culture. While the benefits are manifold in terms of business results, getting there is no small feat.

Volumes have been written on the subject of how to create a team-based culture—a subject that is beyond the scope of this book. In this chapter, we will focus instead on what you as an individual manager or supervisor can do to achieve higher levels of performance by transforming the group of people you are leading into a true team. Obviously, the more the culture of your company or organization is organized around teams, the easier it will be. Even if your company doesn't have a strong team-based culture though, there are still many things you can do to improve the performance results of your work group.

Getting People in Right Relationship

The word *team* is about as American as apple pie and the Star Spangled Banner. Or is it? When we think of *team* we often think of sports. And for those of us who have ever played a team sport, we know the incredible sense of fulfillment that comes from being a part of a team. And then there are our favorite college and professional teams. The seriousness with which many people support their favorite team(s) in this country is truly amazing. If we could harness and direct the energy of team spectators, we could probably cure world hunger.

The flip side of the coin, of course, is that our country is built on rugged individualism and competition—not cooperation and collaboration. When we walk off the playing field, it is every man for himself, especially in the workplace. That is, unless the manager or supervisor of a work group is able to create a different dynamic within the group.

Teams are more important today than ever. Work is more complex; organizations have been flattened, which means most managers are managing many more people; and the rapid speed of change has changed all the rules and made old ways of working obsolete. Most organizations are running on a much leaner staff. Those organizations which create the synergy that comes from teams are usually in a far better competitive position.

A manager or supervisor who is able to create a true sense of team among her work group not only improves performance for the company but creates a whole different work experience for the people. They are able to get a number of personal needs met in addition to the need to pick up a paycheck so they can pay their bills.

A well-known government agency hired us to put all of their managers through an intensive three-day team leadership program over a three-year period. Each session brought a new group of 30 or so managers together to develop ways that they could better lead their teams and ultimately improve service to taxpayers. Those people griping about how the government spends our tax money will be interested to know that we were required to work 12 hours a day in the training sessions which were held in modest accommodations. The policy of this agency was that in order to justify having the program off site, we had to work until 8:30 in the evening, which meant the participants, ourselves included, were exhausted by the end of the day.

Participants attended the session with members of their management team back at work. The whole idea was for the managers of intact groups to create more of a sense of team among themselves so that they could bring the same spirit and ideas back to their work groups. It is amazing the transformation that takes place. As one participant put it on the last day of the program: "You know, when we came here on the first night we were all a little anxious, very reserved, not knowing what to expect. Some of us didn't even know each other. And now, look at us. There is a real sense of community here. It almost feels like family."

The people in the program had worked very hard, but because they were in right relationship with one another and they weren't working in isolation, the work was fun. They were tired but the predominating feeling reported by most of them, ourselves included, was this feeling of camaraderie—the feeling of being connected to other people in a meaningful way. That's the way it is with real work teams. When a group of people make the transition to team, it's almost like magic. People aren't quite sure when or how it happened, all they know is they feel very different and work takes on a new meaning.

How to Create a Team

There are four primary things you must do as a manager in order to create a sense of team. You might think of them as the four legs of a chair.

1. *Give them a common purpose.* Everything should begin and end with the purpose. The purpose is the reason for the team's existence. The purpose provides the focal point for mobilizing the energy of the team members. Without a common purpose, there will be a

hole in the energy bucket. People will perform a lot of tasks, many of which will get you nowhere because there is no focus, no criteria for determining which activities or tasks should be undertaken. If everyone is focused on the purpose, they are more willing to sacrifice their own self-interests for the sake of the team because everyone is ultimately working towards the same goal. The clearer the goal and the more meaningful it is, the easier it will be to get people moving in the same direction.

2. *Get them working together.* In a true team, there is a healthy interdependence between members. Instead of performing as a collection of individuals working on their own, they depend on each other to accomplish clearly defined performance goals. In order to create this kind of interdependence, members of the team must have complementary skills. The more multiskilled the team members, the better.

3. *Develop a common approach for working together.* Team members must have a process for getting to the performance goals. They need a clearly defined strategy and some guidelines for how they will work together to achieve the purpose. There are a lot of ways to skin a cat. The team members, with your help, need to determine how they are going to treat each other, how they will communicate with one another, how the work will flow, etc. The more they define their expectations of one another up front, the more effective they will be.

4. *Hold them mutually and individually accountable for achieving results.* People do what they get rewarded for. If team members aren't held mutually accountable, it is too easy for individuals to revert back to their own self-interests. It must be in the best interest of the individuals to be a good team player. Just like in a sports team, when the team loses, everyone loses. When the team wins, everyone wins. Mutual accountability is what builds commitment and trust.

When these four legs of the chair are in place, you have a solid foundation for creating synergy, which is the whole reason for establishing teams in the first place. Synergy can be defined as the optimal use of the resources that are available. It is a process that surfaces people's diverse ideas, skills, and experiences and integrates them into outcomes that are far more successful than if people were performing as individuals.

Responsibilities of the Manager

When a manager assumes the role of team coach, his responsibilities will depend upon how evolved the team is. At one end of the spectrum, the manager may play a very strong leadership role. At the other end of the spectrum, the team performs many of the functions that were previously performed by the manager. The manager's role is less predominant. In any event, a manager who wishes to take on more of a coaching role and create more of an empowered team must perform the following responsibilities:

- Clarify the team's purpose, team member roles, performance measurements, and boundaries
- Assist the team in setting individual and team goals that are aligned with the larger business goals
- Give directions and refrain from being a judge and jury
- Encourage two-way, open communication
- Support and encourage participation
- Give feedback to the team and individuals on the team
- Determine the training and development needs of the team and the individuals on the team and arrange for training accordingly
- Develop the team's capacity for understanding and dealing with conflict
- Develop decision-making skills of the team so the members are able to make quality decisions which have buy-in from all team members
- Help the team identify and gather the information which is critical to reaching its goals
- Help the team learn to interface effectively with other teams in the organization

A manager who performs as a team coach acts as an advisor, facilitator, and teacher. It's based on the same philosophy we have applied to coaching individuals: the more you support, guide, and influence and the less you tell, control, and demand, the better your people will perform. As with coaching individuals, it only requires that managers unlearn just about everything they have learned about what a manager is supposed to do and how to get results.

A Whole New Set of Skills

It doesn't matter how much technical knowledge or experience people have, unless they can communicate effectively with one another and deal with conflict constructively, they will have great difficulty getting to their goals. Without the necessary interpersonal skills, they are likely to become frustrated and demotivated. In fact, when team members don't have these skills, working in a group can be a very painful experience.

Even when people do have the necessary interpersonal skills, working as a team is still challenging. Every group which becomes a real team must work through some big obstacles together. In fact, it is the owning and overcoming of the obstacles which eventually unites them into a team. Trying to overcome the obstacles and survive as a team without the necessary interpersonal skills is like trying to paddle a canoe without the oars. It simply can't be done.

In order for you to give these skills to your people, you, of course, must possess them yourself. At a minimum, here are the interpersonal skills you and your team will need.

- *Listening skills.* It is through listening that people are able to access the thoughts and ideas of others. When people feel listened to, they often think better because someone is there to receive the thoughts going through their minds. When people are listened to and affirmed, they feel more a part of the group.
- *Conflict resolution.* Whenever people come together to accomplish a goal, conflict is inevitable. The key to resolving conflict effectively is having a positive mindset about it and having the necessary skills to work through it. Most people think of conflict as something negative—something to be avoided. They think conflict is a sign that there is something wrong. Actually, it is quite the opposite. It is an opportunity to grow and learn. Team members need to understand the nature of conflict, where it comes from, and how it can be used to strengthen relationships and achieve a better result. Without this skill, the interests of the individuals will compromise the best interests of the team. The successful resolution of conflict is one of the things that binds team members to one another.
- *Group thinking and decision-making skills.* Effective decisions are those which are of high quality *and* which are accepted and sup-

ported by those who will implement the decision. In order to meet this criteria, team members must have effective interpersonal skills and they must use a rational process in working the problem through to solution. In communicating with one another, they must support one another's ideas, differ with each other in a way that no one feels put down or minimized, and fully participate. The thought process must include an analysis of the situation, the identification of objectives, a full consideration of possible strategies, and a criteria for evaluating the various options. Group thinking and decision-making skills are essential to tapping into and fully utilizing the diversity represented in the group.

Application of The 7 Steps to Trust-Based Management Process

Coaching a team is not that much different from coaching individuals. The process is basically the same. Your relationship with the team as a whole will be the foundation for its performance. The spirit, energy, and competency the leader brings to the team makes all the difference in the world in the members' performance. Here's how The 7 Steps to Trust-Based Management apply.

Step 1: Seek the Truth

In order to understand your team, you should step back frequently and look at the whole. It helps to think of the team almost as a person with certain characteristics, strengths, weaknesses, likes, dislikes, etc. Often we get so focused on tasks and individuals that we don't even think team in our own mind.

When you observe your team, you will do it in much the same way you observe individuals. You'll want to observe and note its performance output as well as its process. How does it get to the results? You should constantly watch for the dynamics that go on between members of the team and the dynamics that transpire between your team and other teams.

There are a number of assessment tools you can use to evaluate how well the individuals in your group are working together. Are they truly a team or simply a collection of individuals? You should also actively solicit feedback from other people and departments and ask them to give you specific examples of how the team behaves and interacts.

Step 2: Give Feedback

In order to reinforce the importance of the individuals working as a team, it's important that you meet with them frequently as a team. In staff meetings, for example, you will want to tell them what you see, think, and feel about how they are performing and working as a team. Speak from the facts, don't criticize, cite examples of what you have observed, be honest and direct, and present a balanced picture of their performance. As you give them your feedback, you should engage them in dialogue. Work on defining the problems and coming up with solutions together. Ask them for feedback on yourself and ask them how you can better support them as a team. And don't forget to affirm them as a team in any way you can.

Step 3: Create a Vision and a Plan

Ask the members how they think they can improve their performance as a team. Help them create a vision of the kind of team they would like to be. With the vision in mind, create a developmental plan which addresses team performance, competencies, and behaviors. Do a gap analysis with them—where they are now in relation to where they want to be. Determine in your own mind what they are unable at this point to see about their performance, competencies, and behaviors. Engage them in establishing action steps and timetables for closing the gaps.

Step 4: Break through Resistance

Sometimes a group of people will band together against the manager as a way of justifying their own actions and performance. Group resistance can often be harder to deal with than individual resistance because of the power of group dynamics. If you feel that happening, don't get defensive or take it personally. The more objective you remain, the more you keep mirroring what you see, and the more you stay on the positive side of the fence, the less reason people will have to band together. If there are one or more naysayers who are stirring up the rest of the group, the more positive you remain, the less power they will have. Sooner or later, the majority of the group will come around. If you go on the attack toward any one individual or the group as a whole, you will in all likelihood lose the entire group.

Step 5: Observe and Mirror

Constantly look for examples of both positive behavior and behavior that needs to be improved which you can mirror back to the team. When you are observing your team, make sure you pay particular attention to the priorities you outlined in the team's developmental plan. In addition to your own observations, make sure you get feedback about the team from outside the group on a regular basis. You especially want to get feedback from the team's customers.

Step 6: Teach and Guide

Be on the lookout for coachable moments at all times. Sometimes it has more impact if you coach members of the team working together on the spot—as close to the time of the event as possible. (That applies to positive events as well.) You don't have to wait for a staff meeting. Remember to keep your feedback free of judgment and criticism at all times. Present it to the team as information that is intended to be helpful. If it is going to be perceived as information, of course, it must be based in fact.

Step 7: Recognize, Celebrate, and Reinforce

Never miss an opportunity to recognize the team as a whole. The more you do, the more the members will begin to see themselves as a team. Don't restrict your recognition to performance results. Reward them when they display the behaviors that make them a well-oiled team. Find unique, creative ways to let the team members know that you sincerely appreciate their efforts, especially when they have accomplished something extraordinary. Make sure you get them the recognition they are due from outside the team. Get their pictures in newsletters, ask higher-level executives to come and thank them personally—anything that gets visibility for them and their achievements.

▼ OUR EXPERIENCE

Stewardship Coaching

Peter Block said that real leaders are "willing to be accountable for the well-being of the larger organization by operating in service, rather than in control, of those around us." I once served on a board of directors of an association of professional speakers where I witnessed this type of leadership firsthand.

The president of the board was a woman who had an amazing leadership style. Leading a group is never easy, but when you factor in the egos that many speakers have, the challenge becomes even greater. On the board were three or four men with particularly large egos and high needs for control. They were constantly speaking out and disagreeing with one another during board meetings which would have been extremely disruptive if not for the skill of our leader. Miraculously, in her quiet, firm way she was able to unite this group into a high-performing team which probably achieved more in terms of membership and quality programming than any chapter before or after.

One of her outstanding qualities was her willingness to let others take center stage. She never took the spotlight when she could give it to someone else. I remember when she asked me to serve on the board, she made me feel so special and important that I could not say no. Throughout the year, she constantly recognized and thanked individuals on the board. She was decisive and kept the group focused on the goals. Those who were not on the board hardly knew who was the force behind our success but we knew and we sang her praises. She has been a role model for me on how to lead teams ever since.

—Diane

Team Coaching Checklist

Here's a checklist to help you determine if you are providing the people you lead with the kind of coaching which unites them into a team.

1. Do you keep the team focused on its purpose at all times?
   Yes ☐   No ☐

2. Have you clearly defined and communicated the team's goals to the members and do you keep them focused as a team?
Yes ☐   No ☐

3. Have you organized the work in such a way that team members are required to work together in order to accomplish the objectives?
Yes ☐   No ☐

4. Have you established with your team a common approach to getting the job done?
Yes ☐   No ☐

5. Do you hold them accountable as a team as well as individually?
Yes ☐   No ☐

6. Have you provided them with the necessary interpersonal skills for working as a team?
Yes ☐   No ☐

7. Have you made sure everyone is clear on their roles and responsibilities?
Yes ☐   No ☐

8. Do you facilitate team decision making?
Yes ☐   No ☐

9. Do you support and encourage full participation on everyone's part?
Yes ☐   No ☐

10. Do you help team members understand and celebrate their differences?
Yes ☐   No ☐

11. Do you observe your team regularly and give them feedback?
Yes ☐   No ☐

12. Do you watch for the formation of factions and are you careful not to react and take things personally?
Yes ☐   No ☐

13. Do you watch for coachable moments?
    Yes ☐   No ☐

14. Do you celebrate their success as a team every time you can?
    Yes ☐   No ☐

15. Are you careful to always give them the credit and resist the temptation to take it for yourself?
    Yes ☐   No ☐

Scoring: If you answered yes to 13 to 15 questions, you probably have a strong team.

If you answered yes to 9 to 12 questions, you are doing a lot of the right things but still have room for improvement in terms of transforming your group into a team.

If you answered yes to fewer than 9 questions, you are probably leading a collection of individuals rather than a team.

PERSONAL ACTION CORNER

Families seem to be so busy today that they have little time to spend together as a unit. Without time spent together, family members can lose their connection and begin to feel that they are simply living under the same roof. Children particularly need a sense of belonging even though their every action seems to say they want to separate from the family. After all, that's their job—to eventually achieve their independence—but not before they are ready.

Something to Try: One of the best ways to maintain a sense of family is to have regular family meetings—a time when family members can check in with one another, express their feelings, and talk about what's on their minds. If you can't get them all together, share with each individual who did not attend what was shared at the meeting. If you have never had such meetings, you may be met with great resistance, particularly from teenagers. Even though they complain, have the meetings anyway and strongly request that everyone attend.

At your first meeting you will want to explain the purpose of the meeting—you can define it anyway you want. You may even let the family members discuss what they would like to address at the meet-

ings. Here are some suggestions for the kinds of things you might want
to do at the meetings.

- Inform people of any upcoming family events and ask if there are
  any conflicts.
- Assign tasks.
- Ask each person what they need from the family that they aren't
  getting.
- Keep them informed on matters that may divide them.
- Encourage openness and do not engage yourself in family gossip.
- Ask each person if he or she has anything to get off his or her
  chest.
- Do not let anyone else speak until the speaker is finished.
- Ask family members how they think the family can operate more
  efficiently.
- Clarify your expectations of the family and give feedback on how
  well they are doing.
- Ask them if they have any feedback for you. Listen and don't de-
  fend yourself until you have had time to think about it.

When people learn skills for communicating and working as a team
at home, they are usually far more successful when they go out into the
work world. The security they feel as a result of being a part of a strong
family unit stays with them the rest of their lives.

Conclusion

Leading people is never easy but it can be very rewarding if you have
the skills and if you bring the right spirit to the job. One of the things
that makes it so challenging is that everyone is different. There are a
thousand and one factors influencing how a person performs, many
over which you have little or no control. What we have tried to provide
in this book is a process for focusing on those factors you can control.

We have suggested a number of things you can do to get high performance from your people but we hope we were successful in communicating one central idea that makes all the "to dos" work. It is the
idea that people work for people, not companies. The quality of the

relationship you have with each person you manage is probably the single most important factor affecting the person's performance and yours.

When we talk about having a quality relationship with your people, we aren't talking about winning a popularity contest. In fact, if you are doing a good job of managing and bringing out the best in your people, you will have some upset along the way. It goes with the territory. As managers, we must give up the desire to always be liked by the people we lead if we are going to serve them well. While people in the workplace are not children and should never be treated as such, there are a number of similarities between managing and parenting and this is one of them.

A quality relationship, of course, is one that is real and authentic— one where truth and honesty are prized above all else. When that is present and people speak the truth for the purpose of helping each other, the team, and ultimately the customer, trust naturally follows. Trust is the bedrock of high performance because when it is present, people stop spending their energies protecting themselves and instead focus their energies on improving their performance.

The same is true in our personal relationships. Honesty breeds trust and trust breeds intimacy. It's that simple, but not always so simple to apply. It takes a fair amount of courage to tell the truth, whether in your personal or work relationships, because most of us have been taught to withhold the truth, tell people what they want to hear, and avoid conflict at all costs. If we all learned the art of delivering feedback so that it helps the other person, our divorce rate would probably plummet, productivity in companies and organizations would skyrocket, and most of all, we would be connected to other people in a much more meaningful way.

No gain, of course, is achieved overnight. It takes commitment and discipline to change old patterns—our own and those of the people we are leading. If you embrace the concepts in this book with your heart as well as your head, we know the benefits will be immeasurable. You will transform your experience of being a manager and the work experience of the people you are leading. If you apply them faithfully at home, the payoff will be even greater. We wish for you all the best.

Further Reading

Albrecht, Karl, *The Northbound Train*. AMACOM, 1994.

Bell, Chip, *Managers as Mentors*. Berrett-Koehler, 1998.

Bellman, Geoffrey, *Getting Things Done When You Are Not In Charge*. Fireside, 1993.

Bennis, Warren, *The Corporate Culture Survival Guide*. Jossey-Bass, 1999.

Blanchard, Ken and Don Shula, *Everyone's a Coach*. HarperBusiness, 1995.

Blanchard, Kenneth, *Gung-Ho: Turn On the People In Any Organization*. William Morrow, 1997.

Brandon, Nathaniel, *Self Esteem at Work*. Jossey-Bass, 1998.

Connellan, Thomas K., *How to Grow People Into Self Starters*. The Achievement Institute, 1991.

Crane, Thomas, *The Heart of Coaching: Using Transformational Coaching to Create a High Performance Culture*. FTA Press, 1998.

Dalton, Maxine and George P. Hollenbeck, *How to Design an Effective System for Developing Managers and Leaders*. The Center for Creative Leadership, 1996.

Davis, James and Adelaide Davis, *Effective Training Strategies: A Comprehensive Guide to Maximizing Learning in Organizations*. Berrett-Koehler, 1998.

Deeprose, Donna, *The Team Coach: Vital New Skills for Supervisors and Managers in a Team Environment*. AMACOM, 1995.

Dotlich, David and Peter Cairo, *Action Coaching: How to Leverage Individual Performance for Company Success*. Jossey-Bass, 1999.

Dotlich, David and James Noel, *Action Learning: How the World's Top Companies Are Re-Creating Their Leaders and Themselves*. Jossey-Bass, 1998.

Doyle, James, *The Business Coach: A Game Plan for the New Work Environment*. Wiley, John & Sons, 1999.

Edwards, Mark, Ph.D, *Providing 360-Degree Feedback: An Approach to Enhancing Individual and Organizational Performance*. American Compensation Association, 1996.

Flaherty, James, *Coaching: Evoking Excellence in Others*. Butterworth-Heinemann, 1998.

Fournies, Ferdinand, *Coaching for Improved Work Performance*. McGraw-Hill, 1999.

Freiberg, Kevin and Jackie and Tom Peters, *NUTS: Southwest Airlines' Crazy Recipe for Business and Personal Success*. Bantam Doubleday Dell, 1998.

Fritts, Patricia, *The New Managerial Mentor: Becoming A Learning Leader to Build Communities of Purpose*. Davies-Black, 1998.

Gilley, Jerry and Nathanial Boughton, *Stop Managing, Start Coaching*. McGraw-Hill, 1996.

Goldsmith, Marshall and Francis Hesselbein, *Leading Beyond the Walls*. Jossey-Bass, 1999.

Goleman, Daniel, *Emotional Intelligence*. Bantam Books, 1997.

Goleman, Daniel, *Working with Emotional Intelligence*. Bantam, 1998.

Hargrove, Robert, *Mastering the Art of Creative Collaboration*. McGraw-Hill, 1998.

Hargrove, Robert, *Masterful Coaching*. Jossey-Bass, 1995.

Harris, Jim, Ph.D., *Getting Employees to Fall in Love with Your Company*. AMACOM, 1996.

Hendricks, William, *Coaching, Mentoring and Managing*. Career Press, 1996.

Huang, Chungliang Al, and Jerry Lynch, *Mentoring: The Tao of Giving and Receiving Wisdom*. HarperCollins, 1995.

Hudson, Frederic, *The Handbook of Coaching: A Comprehensive Resource Guide for Managers, Executives, Consultants, and HR.* Jossey-Bass, 1999.

Johnson, Harold, *Mentoring for Exceptional Performance.* Griffin, 1997.

Jones, Bearley, *360-Degree Feedback: Strategies, Tactics and Techniques.* Human Resource Development Press, 1996.

Kaplan, Robert and Charles Paulus, *Enhancing 360-Degree Feedback for Senior Executives: How to Maximize the Benefits and Minimize the Risks.* Center for Creative Leadership, 1994.

Kaye, Beverly and Sharon Jordan-Evans, *Love 'Em or Lose 'Em: Getting Good People to Stay.* Berrett-Koehler, 1999.

Kilburg, Richard, *Executive Coaching: Developing Managerial Wisdom in a World of Chaos.* American Psychological Association, 2000.

Kinlaw, Dennis, *Coaching for Commitment: Interpersonal Strategies for Obtaining Superior Performance from Individuals and Teams.* Jossey-Bass, 1999.

Kinlaw, Dennis and Richard Roe, *Coaching: The ASTD Trainer's Sourcebook.* McGraw-Hill, 1995.

Knowles, Malcolm, *The Adult Learner: A Neglected Species.* Gulf Publishing, 1990.

Kushel, Gerald, *The Fully Effective Executive.* AMACOM, 1991.

Kushel, Gerald, *Reaching the Peak Performance Zone.* AMACOM, 1994.

Marshall, Edward, *Building Trust at the Speed of Change: The Power of the Relationship-Based Corporation.* AMACOM, 1999.

Mink, Oscar G., *Developing High Performance People: The Art of Coaching.* Perseus, 1993.

Mitroff, Ian, and Elisabeth Denton, *Spiritual Audit of Corporate America.* Jossey-Bass, 1999.

Murray, Margo, *Beyond the Myths and Magic of Mentoring.* Jossey-Bass, 1991.

O'Neill, Mary Beth, *Executive Coaching with Backbone and Heart: A Systems Approach to Engaging Leaders with Their Challenges.* Jossey-Bass, 2000.

Peterson, David, Ph.D. and Mary Dee Hicks, Ph.D., *Development First: Strategies for Self Development.* Personnel Decisions International, 1995.

Peterson, David, Ph.D and Mary Dee Hicks, Ph.D., *The Leader as Coach.* Personnel Decisions International, 1996.

Schutz, William, *The Human Element: Productivity, Self Esteem and the Bottom Line.* Jossey-Bass, 1999.

Senge, Peter, *The Fifth Discipline.* Doubleday, 1990.

Stone, Douglas, *Difficult Conversations: How to Discuss What Matters Most.* Penguin USA, 2000.

Warner, Alan, *Change and the Bottom Line.* Ashgate Publishing, 1997.

Weyant, Bob, *Confronting Without Guilt or Conflict.* Brassy Publishing, 1995.

Whitmore, John, *Coaching for Performance (People Skills for Professionals).* Nickolas Brealy, 1996.

Whitney, John O., *Power Plays: Shakespeare's Lessons in Leadership and Management.* Simon and Schuster, 2000.

Whitney, John O., *The Economics of Trust: Liberating Profits and Restoring Corporate Vitality.* McGraw-Hill, 1995.

Whitworth, Laura, Henry House, and Phil Sandahl, *Co-Active Coaching: New Skills for Coaching People Toward Success in Work and Life.* Davies-Black, 1998.

Witherspoon, Robert and Randall White, *Four Essential Ways Coaches Help Executives.* Center for Creative Leadership, 1997.

For information on developing competencies:
Exxceed, Inc.
35 East Wacker Drive, Suite 500
Chicago, Illinois 60601
m.zwell@Exxceed.com

Index